MELTDOWN

MELTDOWN

A Free-Market Look at Why the Stock Market Collapsed,
the Economy Tanked, and Government Bailouts
Will Make Things Worse

THOMAS E. WOODS JR.

Since 1947
REGNERY
PUBLISHING, INC.
An Eagle Publishing Company • Washington, DC

Cataloging-in-Publication data on file with the Library of Congress

ISBN 978-1-59698-587-2

Published in the United States by
Regnery Publishing, Inc.
One Massachusetts Avenue, NW
Washington, DC 20001
www.regnery.com

Manufactured in the United States of America

10 9 8 7 6 5 4 3 2 1

Books are available in quantity for promotional or premium use. Write to Director of Special Sales, Regnery Publishing, Inc., One Massachusetts Avenue NW, Washington, DC 20001, for information on discounts and terms or call (202) 216-0600.

Distributed to the trade by:
Perseus Distribution
387 Park Avenue South
New York, NY 10016

To Murray N. Rothbard (1926–1995) and Ron Paul,
who told the truth

Contents

FOREWORD BY
CONGRESSMAN RON PAUL

Many Americans are looking to the new administration to solve our economic problems. Unfortunately, that is probably a vain hope. Although we were promised "change," we are likely to get a continuation of the same superficial economic fixes that have damaged so many economies in the past, and that will only delay the return of prosperity.

These fixes are based on the false belief that the free-market economy has failed. But it is not the market that has failed. It is intervention into the market that has failed. The Federal Reserve and its manipulation of money and interest rates have failed. None of this can be blamed on the free market, but that isn't stopping newspaper columnists from doing so anyway.

Keynesian so-called economists, led by Paul Krugman, are vainly reaching into their usual bag of tricks to try to solve the problems of intervention with more intervention, and nothing is working. But they are persistent. They'll keep scrounging around in that bag all throughout the

Obama administration. The slump will continue, since none of these tricks has the slightest thing to do with the underlying problems in the economy. All we'll have to show for them is an empty Keynesian bag and a lot more unpayable debt.

Meanwhile, who's being ignored during this crisis? The free-market economists of the Austrian School of economic thought, *the very people who predicted not only the Great Depression, but also the calamity we're dealing with today.* The good news is that Austrian School economists are gaining more acceptance every day, and have a greater chance of influencing our future than they've had for a long time. I'm told that Google searches for "Austrian economics" are off the charts.

We can probably expect an avalanche of books in the coming months that purport to tell us what happened to the economy and what we should do about it. They'll be dead wrong, and most of the advice they provide will be dreadful. You can count on that.

That's why *Meltdown* is so important. This book actually gets things right. It correctly identifies our problems, their causes, and what we should do about them. It treats the architects of this debacle not with the undeserved reverence they receive in Washington and on television, but with the critical eye that is so conspicuously missing from our supposedly independent thinkers in academia and the media. Tom Woods reserves his admiration for those few who, unlike the quacks who would instruct us now, actually saw the crisis coming, have a theory to explain it, and can show us the way out.

In a short span, Tom introduces the layman to a range of subjects that have been excluded from our national discussion for much too long. Topics our opinion leaders thought they'd buried forever, or never heard of in the first place, are suddenly back, and not a moment too soon. This book is an indispensable conduit of these critical ideas. Among many other things, Tom explains Austrian business cycle theory, which he correctly identifies as the single most important piece of economic knowledge for Americans to have right now. In so doing, Tom provides Americans with the most persuasive and rational account of how we got here. Only if we correctly assess the causes of the debacle can we hope to propose a path to recovery that might actually work and not simply prolong the agony.

Our years of living beyond our means, of buying everything on credit and on money printed out of thin air, are over. Sure, our government will carry on with its nonsensical policy of curing indebtedness with more indebtedness, inflation with more inflation, but the game is up. It's not going to work. What are they going to do when the entitlement crisis hits and the federal government is suddenly on the hook for tens of trillions of dollars? If they try to print their way out of that one, they'll destroy the dollar for good, if they haven't done so already with all these bailouts. The resources aren't there. It's time we recognized this like adults and adjusted our behavior accordingly. The more we intervene and the more we prop up economic zombies, the worse off we'll be. But the sooner we understand what has happened, assess our economic situation honestly, and rebuild our economy on a sound foundation, the sooner our fortunes will be restored.

Ideas still matter, and sound economic education has rarely been as urgently necessary as it is today. There is no better book to read on the present crisis than this one, and that is why I am delighted to endorse and introduce it.

—*The Honorable Ron Paul, member of Congress*

CHAPTER 1

THE ELEPHANT
IN THE LIVING ROOM

Since the fall of 2008, as the stock market plummeted, companies folded, and economic fear and uncertainty began to spread, Americans have been bombarded with a predictable and relentless refrain: the free-market economy has failed.

The remedy? According to Barack Obama, the late Bush Administration, Republicans and Democrats in Congress, and the mainstream media, it's more regulation, more government intervention, more spending, more money creation, and more debt.

To add insult to injury, the very people who devised the policies that produced the mess are now posing as the wise public servants who will show us the way out. Following a familiar pattern, government failure has been blamed on anyone and everyone but the government itself. And of course, that same government failure is being used to justify further increases in government power.

The talking heads have been about their usual business of giving the wrong answers to every important question, but this time most of them haven't even been asking the right questions. Where did all the excess risk, leverage, and debt, not to mention the housing bubble itself, come from? When questions like this are raised, the answers are, to say the least, unhelpful. "Excessive risk-taking" simply begs the question. As several economists have noted, blaming the crisis on "greed" is like blaming plane crashes on gravity.

We've been looking in the wrong place. The current crisis was caused not by the free market but by the government's intervention in the market. This is not special pleading on behalf of the market, but the clear verdict of both theory and experience. Fannie Mae and Freddie Mac, government-sponsored enterprises (GSEs) that enjoy various government privileges alongside their special tax and regulatory breaks, were able to draw far more resources into the housing sector than would have been possible on the free market. For years, congressional Democrats pretended all was well at Fannie and Freddie, and that all the warnings were coming from mean people who didn't want the poor to have a chance to own their own homes. (Numerous Democrats really did say that, believe it or not.) Republicans have since used the Democrats' sorry record as a bludgeon against them, but their own record on spending, debt, and government intervention is nothing to be proud of. Republicans by and large have also supported the endless march of government bailouts, which aren't exactly examples of the free market in action.

But even many of those who describe themselves as supporters of the free market have failed to grasp the heart of the problem. To be sure, they have pinpointed legislation like the Community Reinvestment Act that certainly didn't help matters. In pointing fingers at specific programs, however, Republicans have diverted attention to the patient's runny nose and away from his cancer.

Almost nobody in Washington, and precious few elsewhere, has been willing to question the greatest single government intervention in the economy, and the institution whose fingerprints are all over our current mess: America's central bank, the Federal Reserve System. The Fed is hardly ever mentioned in connection with the crisis, except perhaps as our savior. Major newspapers, magazines, and websites purport to dissect the crisis and identify its causes without mentioning the Fed at all. That's nothing new: there has been no serious discussion of the Federal Reserve in public life for the nearly one hundred years since its creation. The Fed is a wonderful thing, and that's that.

When President George W. Bush addressed the nation on September 24, 2008, with the proposed bailout plan for the financial sector meeting stiff resistance from the American public, he devoted some time to addressing what were purportedly the downturn's "root causes." Apart from a fleeting and ambiguous reference to Fannie Mae and Freddie Mac, none of these implicated the government or its central bank. One of the rules of American political life is that inflationary monetary policy by the Fed is never to be mentioned as the source of any of the country's problems, much less the cause of the boom-bust business cycle. The president stuck to the script: not a single word about the central bank.

Several weeks later, the President announced his intention to hold an international summit in Washington on the financial crisis. (As investment advisor Mike Shedlock put it, "In response to the credit crisis President Bush is gathering up all the people who did not see what was coming, denied what was happening, and then failed to see the implications of what was indeed happening."[1]) He spoke of the need to "preserve the foundations of democratic capitalism," the usual boilerplate whenever the federal government intends another round of burdens on the free market. Various presidents and prime ministers were invited.

The response was predictably inane. Upon hearing of the proposed summit, the French president and the European Commission president indicated their desire to see offshore tax havens targeted, the International Monetary Fund further empowered, and limitations imposed on executive pay, among other irrelevant suggestions. As usual, the possibility that artificially low interest rates of 1 percent might have set the world's economies on unsustainable paths was not mentioned then or at the November 15 summit itself, which wound up being a relatively tooth-less exchange of platitudes.[2]

In October 2008 the editor in chief of the Slate Group, which pub-lishes *Slate*, the popular website, proclaimed that the financial crisis was surely the end of libertarianism, since it supposedly proved what a mess "unregulated markets" could cause. Not once were central banking or the Federal Reserve mentioned, even though these are not creations of the free market and their destructive behavior is not the market's fault.

To be sure, a few important exceptions to this general rule can be found, such as investment mavens Jim Rogers, Peter Schiff, and James Grant. Rogers, when asked on CNBC what two courses of action he would take if he were appointed Fed chairman, replied that he would abolish the Fed and then resign. Not by coincidence, these men were also among the very few who predicted the current crisis. So-called main-stream commentators, whose credibility should have completely evapo-rated by now, laughed at their pessimistic predictions and their criticisms of Fed policy. Thanks to YouTube, you can watch a parade of blockheads actually laughing at Peter Schiff in 2006 for predicting exactly what has happened since. As predictably as night follows day, the dopes who didn't see the crisis coming and said everything was fine are the ones George W. Bush and Barack Obama alike have looked to for advice on how to reverse it.

We are in trouble.

More bailouts, more regulation, more government

The government's course of action in the face of the sinking economy has been just as predictable. First, government officials misdiagnosed the problem, exonerating themselves of any blame and pinpointing various bogeymen instead. For guidance, they turned to studying the causes and cures of the Great Depression—which they of course got all wrong. Then they drew an analogy between (their misinterpretation of) the current sit-uation and (their misinterpretation of) the Great Depression.

Next, Americans were told that in order to prevent another Great Depression, the government had no choice but to implement the same policies that failed to lift the country out of the actual Great Depression. Finally, it was time for our wise rulers to set about making things worse, beginning with (but not confining themselves to) a massive and unprecedented string of bailouts. Depressed economic conditions will thereby persist longer than they would have if the market had been allowed to function.

When in September 2008 the House of Representatives entertained a $700 billion bailout package—soon to be renamed the "rescue plan" by the Bush administration and its media accomplices—for the financial sector, the public response was swift and clear. Democratic senator Barbara Boxer of California reported receiving nearly 17,000 e-mail messages on the subject, nearly all of them negative. Of more than 2,000 calls to her California office (on a single day), only 40 callers supported it—that's 2 percent. Out of 918 calls to her Washington office, exactly one was in favor. Other members of Congress reported similar reactions. Ohio senator Sherrod Brown reported that 95 percent of constituent communications on the subject were from bailout opponents.[3]

What could make a representative disregard so intense an expression of outrage on the part of his constituents? Take a wild guess. The securities and investment industry, according to the Center for Responsive Politics, contributed $53 million to congressional and presidential candidates in the 2008 cycle, placing them second behind lawyers. Congressmen who voted in favor of the bailout when it appeared before the House on September 29 had received 54 percent more money in campaign contributions from banks and securities firms than had those who voted against it.[4]

Surprisingly, the House voted it down at first. That could not be allowed to stand. Instead of concluding that the population did not want the bailout, legislators got to work to figure out how the bill could still be rammed through. The Senate version included billions of dollars' worth of the usual targeted enticements, and the bill was promptly passed and signed into law. Sure, looting the American population to the tune of $700 billion in order to bail out the most reckless actors on Wall Street seemed like a bad idea, but now that we've added a $6 million tax break for makers of children's wooden arrows, well, that's another story.

After the bailout passed, Treasury secretary Henry Paulson did not exactly comport himself like a man in command of events. First we were told that the bailout money would buy up bad assets from banks (like nonperforming mortgages and "toxic" mortgage-backed securities), and thus revive interbank lending, which had dropped off because of the banks' uncertainty surrounding other banks' exposure to these assets. The administration, congressional leaders, and the media all hammered away against doubters and dissenters that this was the right plan, and it was needed now.

But after the bill passed they changed their minds. The strategy of buying up bad assets was first postponed in favor of handing government money to the banks in exchange for shares of bank stock, even if the banks weren't willing to sell. Then bad-asset purchases were finally abandoned, expressly, by Secretary Paulson. The strategy that we had all been told was critical to the economy, and that we would suffer a collapse of historic proportions without, was simply and promptly forgotten. Paulson even admitted later on that he had known from the beginning that such a strategy—on the basis of which the bailout package was sold to the public—was the wrong solution.[5]

Now it was consumer credit that needed propping up. According to Paulson, "millions of Americans" were facing rising credit card rates or reduced access to credit, thus "making it more expensive for families to finance everyday purchases." That made even less sense than the usual Paulson rationalization. Think about it: is it sustainable in the long run for families to make everyday purchases on credit? How can that go on? Yet we are being asked to prop up an obviously unsustainable system based on borrowing and consumption, instead of encouraging people to live within their means as the market is now trying to do. One doesn't normally look to government officials for economic understanding, but

German chancellor Angela Merkel correctly warned in November 2008 that if Washington's policy was to create more money and encourage more borrowing, it would simply sow "the seeds of a similar crisis in five years' time."[6]

The two major-party candidates for president in 2008 agreed on the congressional bailout package, of course—Americans can't be permitted a real choice on a matter as important as that. Thanks to bailout mania, by the end of 2008 Washington had put itself (meaning the American population) on the hook for some $7.7 trillion. And all indications are that they're just getting started.

"Change you can believe in"

A first glance at Barack Obama's economic team confirms that all the talk of "change" really meant more of the same—more bailouts, more government intervention, more addressing symptoms rather than causes—along with huge deficits and massive increases in government spending, which our leaders superstitiously believe can restore economic health. As with any superstition, no amount of logical argument or historical evidence seems able to dislodge it. This one is particularly difficult to overturn, since it gives intellectual cover to additional spending, something government likes to engage in anyway.

All of these imagined masters of the universe—Henry Paulson, Ben Bernanke, Barack Obama, congressional chairmen like Barney Frank and Chris Dodd—should leave well enough alone. There is nothing the government or the Federal Reserve can do to improve the situation, and a great deal they can do to prolong it. As I suggest in this book, they already have.

We cannot expect the situation to improve until we understand how we got here.

No novel theories are necessary. In these pages I provide a layman's overview of where the economy is and what should be done next, and call attention to a range of important ideas that have been ignored for far too long. A free-market perspective—specifically, the ideas of Ludwig von Mises and F. A. Hayek—sheds important light on the crisis we currently face, a crisis even many economists and financial analysts do not fully understand, and which is accounted for adequately by none of the usual theories. The ideas in this book are, for the most part, old ones. They've simply been neglected.

The Fed

Interviewed by the *New York Times* in early November 2008, economist James K. Galbraith claimed that perhaps 10 or 12 of the country's 15,000 professional economists saw the economic crisis coming.[7] Well, few of the economists Galbraith associates with may have seen it coming, but hundreds of economists who belong to Mises' Austrian School of economic thought sure saw it. The Austrian School is a small but growing school of free-market economics whose distinguished lineage includes Mises (1881–1973) and Nobel Laureate Hayek (1899–1992). By and large the Austrians warned of the housing bubble before anyone else, and they predicted the crash the economy is enduring now. And the primary culprit, from their point of view, is the Federal Reserve.

Pretense aside, the Federal Reserve System is for all intents and purposes an arm of the federal government. Created by an act of Congress, its chairman chosen by government appointment, and endowed with monopoly privileges, the Fed rests on principles diametrically opposed to those of the free market. It is dedicated to central economic planning, the great discredited idea of the twentieth century. Except instead of planning the production of steel and concrete, as in the old Soviet Union, it plans money and interest rates, with consequences that necessarily reverberate throughout the economy.

The Fed's policy of intervening in the economy to push interest rates lower than the market would have set them was the single greatest contributor to the crisis that continues to unfold before us. Making cheap credit available for the asking does encourage excessive leverage, speculation, and indebtedness. Manipulating interest rates and thereby misleading investors about real economic conditions does in fact misdirect capital into unsustainable lines of production and discombobulate the market. Imagine that.

As we'll see, the Fed's intervention into the economy can give rise to the boom-bust cycle, making us feel prosperous until we suffer the inevitable crash. The free market is inevitably blamed for that crash. No one even thinks to point the finger at Washington and the Fed. And that is part of what makes it so insidious. These artificial booms, wrote economist Henry Hazlitt decades ago, must end "in a crisis and a slump, and . . . worse than the slump itself may be the public delusion that the slump has been caused, not by the previous inflation, but by the inherent defects of 'capitalism.'"[8]

The Fed is the elephant in the living room that everyone pretends not to notice. Even many of those who blame government for the current mess leave the Fed out of the picture altogether. The free market, meanwhile, takes the blame for the destructive consequences of what it does. This charade has gone on long enough. It's time to consider the possibility that maybe the elephant, and not little Johnny, is the one breaking all the furniture.

CHAPTER 2

HOW GOVERNMENT CREATED THE HOUSING BUBBLE

Everyone remembers the hype. *A house is the best investment you can make. Houses never lose value. Getting rid of down payments will help create an "ownership society." Flipping houses is a great way to make lots of money.*

So much for that.

How far will housing prices fall? More in some markets than in others, but the fall could be substantial. When Japan's housing bubble burst, home prices declined by an average of 80 percent.

As we'll see, the authorities assured us that such a thing could never happen. Rising house prices weren't a bubble, and couldn't be popped. Real estate is all local anyway, so prices could never decline across the country.

These are the same people we're expected to listen to today.

What went wrong? The crisis began when mortgage defaults began a substantial and unexpected increase, triggering a chain reaction throughout the entire financial sector. The standard account has explained the *mechanics* of what happened more or less correctly, but has done a poor job of accounting for the ultimate causes of the housing crash.

What happened?

From 1998 to 2006, home prices appreciated dramatically. In some markets, prices for even the most modest dwellings became astronomically high. This rise in prices spurred still more home building, and the resulting glut of houses finally began to put downward pressure on prices. Housing prices started to fall beginning in the third quarter of 2006. Until that time, people having trouble making their mortgage payments had been able to sell their homes, confident that they had appreciated, or even just to refinance them. These options were disappearing for borrowers experiencing difficulties.

The bursting of the housing bubble had repercussions far beyond the world of mortgage lenders and homeowners. The financial system had invested heavily in mortgage-backed securities. Traditionally, a homeowner took out a mortgage at his local bank and made his monthly mortgage payments to that institution. More recently, banks have been able to sell these mortgages on what is called the secondary mortgage market to institutions like Fannie Mae (more on them below), which then are entitled to receive the monthly mortgage payments associated with them. Fannie, in turn, bundles many of these mortgages together and markets them as mortgage-backed securities. When an investor buys one, he his buying a share of the pool of income that results from all the mortgage payments homeowners make on these mortgages every month. The advantage of these securities was thought to be their diversification of risk. In other words, because they consisted of mortgages drawn from housing markets all over the U.S., they were to that degree protected against unexpected downturns in the housing sector in one part of the country. These mortgage eggs were placed in many different geographic baskets, as it were.

But what if the housing market in the *entire country* should suffer an unexpected slump and mortgage foreclosures should increase? In that case, as we have seen since 2006, holders of mortgage-backed securities find themselves in trouble. As foreclosures have increased and more people have defaulted on their mortgages, the stream of mortgage payments associated with these securities has become lower than investors expected when they purchased them. These securities go down in value, as do the companies that own them.

One of the scandals associated with mortgage-backed securities is that the ratings agencies, whose task it is to assess the level of risk associated with various securities, assigned these assets a very high rating, often AAA. Owners of these assets, who thought they were investing their money safely and conservatively, had in fact exposed themselves to much more risk than the ratings agencies were letting on.

Blaming "greedy lenders" or even foolish borrowers for what happened merely begs the question. What institutional factors gave rise to all the foolish lending and borrowing in the first place? Why did the banks have so much money available to lend in the mortgage market—so much indeed that they could throw it even at applicants who lacked jobs, income, down payment money, and good credit? These phenomena, as well as the housing bubble and the economic crisis more generally, are consistently traceable to government intervention in the economy.

Culprit 1: Fannie Mae and Freddie Mac

At the center of the collapse were the Federal National Mortgage Association and the Federal Home Loan Mortgage Corporation, better known as Fannie Mae and Freddie Mac. These leviathan corporations are creatures of Congress and are officially known as "government-sponsored enterprises" or GSEs. What do they do? Fannie and Freddie do not extend mortgage loans to home buyers. They buy loans from banks on what is called the secondary market. In other words, after a bank offers a home loan to a consumer, it can sell that loan to Fannie or

Freddie. From that moment on, the loan is no longer on the books of the originating bank and Fannie or Freddie becomes responsible for it, both receiving the stream of monthly payments it represents and bearing the risk associated with the possibility that the homeowner could default. Fannie and Freddie might hold these mortgages in their own portfolios, but they often would bundle them into mortgage-backed securities for sale to investors.

Meanwhile, the originating bank, having divested itself of this mortgage by selling to Fannie or Freddie, now has the funds to go back into the mortgage market and extend another loan to a new consumer. The whole process spurs more mortgage lending than would otherwise have taken place, making it easier for people to buy homes. This artificial diversion of resources into mortgage lending inflates home prices. It is artificial because this secondary mortgage market is fueled largely by the special privileges Fannie and Freddie have been granted by government.

Fannie Mae was originally created as a government agency during the New Deal of the 1930s, and was privatized in 1968. Freddie was created as a putatively private competitor in 1970. As GSEs, their exact status as public or private entities has always been ambiguous—they enjoy special tax and regulatory privileges that potential competitors do not, but their stock is traded on the New York Stock Exchange. Their securities are designated as "government securities" and can be held by banks as low-risk bonds. And for years, Fannie has had a special $2.25 billion line of credit with the U.S. Treasury.

Most important, investors and lenders took for granted that if Fannie needed it, this line of credit would be essentially unlimited. Everybody knew that if the GSEs ran into trouble, they would be bailed out at taxpayer expense. (Everybody was proven correct when the Treasury placed these companies into "conservatorship" in 2008—the federal government essentially took them over, as we'll see in chapter 5.) For years, this implicit bailout guarantee made it possible for the companies to raise money from investors more readily, and make higher offers for mortgages from banks than any competitor could. And although Fannie and Freddie had been minor players in the mortgage market until the 1990s, on the eve of the federal government takeover in 2008 they had a hand in about half the country's mortgages, and nearly three-quarters of new mortgages.

Fannie was also deeply involved in the politically instigated move to lower lending requirements in the name of helping "disadvantaged" groups. In September 1999, the *New York Times* reported that Fannie Mae was easing credit requirements on the mortgages it bought from banks. The initiative, the *Times* said, would encourage banks "to extend home mortgages to individuals whose credit is generally not good enough to qualify for conventional loans." Fannie Mae had been "under increasing pressure from the Clinton Administration to expand mortgage loans among low and moderate income people."[1] Although "the new mortgages [would] be extended to all potential borrowers who can qualify for a mortgage," one of the program's goals was to "increase the number of minority and low-income home owners who [tended] to have worse credit ratings than non-Hispanic whites."[2] Even the *Times* understood the risk involved: "In moving, even tentatively, into this new area of lending, Fannie Mae is taking on significantly more risk, which may not pose any difficulties during flush economic times. But the government-subsidized corporation may run into trouble in an economic downturn, prompting a government rescue similar to that of the savings and loan industry in the 1980s."

Fannie and Freddie, meanwhile, continued to build up ever-riskier obligations. Congressional Republicans, in turn, called for greater regulation and oversight of Fannie and Freddie. Congressional Democrats balked, claiming that concerns about the mortgage giants were really just a concealed Republican attack on "affordable housing" itself. More cynical observers suspected a different reason for Democratic reluctance to scrutinize Fannie: run by prominent Democrats for years and increasingly a reliable source of Democratic campaign contributions, Fannie was better left alone. It was, critics alleged, a Democratic Party piggy bank, with former

Clinton budget director Franklin Raines walking away with the grand prize, pocketing $100 million in compensation in his brief stint there.

Short of simply abolishing Fannie and Freddie and allowing mortgage lending to take place on a rational, non-politicized basis, greater oversight was certainly desirable, since the public (as it turns out) was on the hook for the companies' losses. This was no purely private corporation that would have to bear the full brunt of its losses should it take on unnecessary risk. But it wasn't to be. According to the *New York Times*, congressional Democrats feared that "tighter regulation of the companies could sharply reduce their commitment to financing low-income and affordable housing." Speaking in September 2003, Democratic congressman Barney Frank of Massachusetts declared that Fannie and Freddie were "not facing any kind of financial crisis.... The more people exaggerate these problems, the more pressure there is on these companies, the less we will see in terms of affordable housing."[3] Congressman Ron Paul of Texas, on the other hand, in testimony before the House Financial Services Committee on September 10, 2003, warned of the destructive consequences for the U.S. economy that Fannie and Freddie would have:

> The special privileges granted to Fannie and Freddie have distorted the housing market by allowing them to attract capital they could not attract under pure market conditions. As a result, capital is diverted from its most productive use into housing. This reduces the efficacy of the entire market and thus reduces the standard of living of all Americans.
>
> Despite the long-term damage to the economy inflicted by the government's interference in the housing market, the government's policy of diverting capital to other uses creates a short-term boom in housing. Like all artificially created bubbles, the boom in housing prices cannot last forever. When housing prices fall, homeowners will experience difficulty as their equity is wiped out. Furthermore, the holders of the mortgage debt will

also have a loss. These losses will be greater than they would have otherwise been had government policy not actively encouraged overinvestment in housing.

Amid repeated warnings like this, Democrats in Congress continued to shelter Fannie from oversight, and Republican leadership took no action.

Culprit 2: The Community Reinvestment Act and affirmative action in lending

Fannie and Freddie weren't the only entities in Washington pushing for looser lending requirements. Government agencies of various kinds were pressuring lenders into making riskier loans in the name of "racial equality." Not wanting to be on the wrong end of lawsuits demanding hundreds of millions in damages, these lenders did as they were told.

Charges of racial discrimination in lending helped spur this rush. In 1992, a study by the Federal Reserve Bank of Boston claimed to find evidence that even allowing for differences in creditworthiness, minority applicants were still getting mortgage loans at lower rates than whites. That study was widely hailed as definitive by those who wanted to believe its conclusions, that American banks were guilty of discrimination against blacks and Hispanics (though not against Asians, who got mortgage loans at even higher rates than whites), and should be forced to make credit more widely available to people in inner-city neighborhoods. Evidence later surfaced exposing the sloppiness of the study, and showing that no evidence of discrimination was found when errors in the data were corrected, but it was too late. The pressure groups had their bludgeon and intended to use it.

The Community Reinvestment Act (CRA), a Jimmy Carter–era law that was given new life by the Clinton administration, has received a great deal of attention and criticism since the housing bust began. That law opened banks up to crushing discrimination suits if they did not lend to minorities in numbers high enough to satisfy the authorities. But it wasn't just the CRA that was pushing lower lending standards. It was the entire political establishment. And according to the University of Texas's Stan Liebowitz, one thing a scan of the housing literature from 1990 until 2006 will *not* yield is any suggestion that "perhaps these weaker lending standards that every government agency involved with housing tried to advance, that Congress tried to advance, that the presidency tried to advance, that the GSEs tried to advance—and with which the penitent banks initially went along and eventually supported with enthusiasm—might lead to high defaults, particularly if housing prices should stop rising."[4]

Shortly after its discrimination study was published, the Boston Fed also released a manual for banks on nondiscriminatory mortgage lending. It explained that banks would have trouble attracting business from minority customers if its lending criteria contained "arbitrary or unreasonable measures of creditworthiness." We can safely assume that banks did not need to be told that "arbitrary or unreasonable measures of creditworthiness" were bad for the banking business. What the Boston Fed really meant, of course, was that the bank's standards were clearly "arbitrary or unreasonable" if minority customers were not receiving a significant percentage of the bank's loans. The rest of the manual was filled with the same kind of politically correct doublespeak—about credit history, down payments, and traditional sources of income, all of which were presented as dispensable obstacles in the way of increased homeownership among society's least advantaged.[5]

Naturally, banks did what government regulators wanted them to do. "Banks began to loosen lending standards," says Liebowitz. "And loosen and loosen, to the cheers of the politicians, regulators, and GSEs."[6] Bear Stearns, a major underwriter of mortgage-backed securities, argued for the soundness of these mortgages on the same Orwellian grounds as the Boston Fed. The credit rating of a borrower shouldn't be so important, their literature explained. "CRA loans do not fit neatly into the standard credit score framework."[7] And so on through the whole roster of traditional lending standards.

In the face of the housing meltdown, supporters of the CRA tried to claim that since the Act applied only to depository institutions (banks, such as Bank of America) and that most of the unsound mortgage lending took place outside such institutions (more specialized mortgage lenders such as Countrywide), the CRA was exonerated from blame. What they didn't say was that the same cavalier approach to risk assessment that informed the CRA pervaded the whole mortgage-lending arena, thanks to the other agencies that pushed the same destructive, loose-lending strategy on all American financial institutions: Fannie and Freddie, the Department of Housing and Urban Development (more on which below), the Federal Reserve, and others, as well as additional legislation like the Equal Credit Opportunity Act.

Henry Cisneros, Bill Clinton's first secretary of the Department of Housing and Urban Development (HUD), loosened lending restrictions both while in government and in his own ventures in the private sector to make it possible for people to buy houses who would not have qualified for mortgage loans in the past. He became a developer himself, joining with KB Home, on whose board he served, to build some 428 homes for low-income buyers in the Lago Vista development in San Antonio.[8]

But even Cisneros had to admit that whatever his good intentions, "people came to homeownership who should not have been homeowners." The *New York Times*, which sympathizes with his politics, says Cisneros

> encouraged the unprepared to buy homes—part of a broad national trend with dire economic consequences. He reflects often on his role in the debacle, he says, which has changed homeownership from something that secured a place in the middle class to something that is ejecting people from it. "I've been waiting for someone to put all the blame at my doorstep," he says lightly, but with a bit of worry, too.

Cisneros is the very model of the public-spirited advocate for the little guy whose paternal oversight is supposed to protect us from the ravages of the free market, and in whom we are expected to place our confidence in the future, when "free-market capitalism" will be more heavily regulated. Cisneros personified the federal government's ambition to expand homeownership, which by his own admission meant lowering lending standards and qualifying people for mortgages who would not have qualified in the past. And yet Cisneros sounded no warnings at all about the mortgage market, and did nothing to discourage subprime lending when he returned to the private sector. His own development company, American CityVista, partnered with KB, where he already served on the board—right alongside James A. Johnson, former Fannie Mae CEO. Fannie guaranteed many of the mortgages in the KB/CityVista orbit. Fannie's top client was Countrywide. Cisneros served on that board as well, and sat by in silence as Countrywide vigorously pushed subprime mortgages. There can be little doubt that Cisneros supported the expansion of subprimes; how else, after all, could his ambitious plans for "expanding homeownership" have been achieved?

Victor Ramirez, who bought a home in Lago Vista in 2002, told the *Times*, "I was a student making $17,000 a year, my wife was between jobs. In retrospect, how in hell did we qualify?" Most residents, he says, were "duped into believing it was easier than it was. The attitude was, 'Sign here, sign here, don't read the fine print.'" Ramirez wouldn't go so far as to say people were victimized; "we were definitely willing victims," he admitted.

As for more "regulation" as the solution—as if regulators could forcibly prevent people from taking out foolish home equity loans, for instance—Cisneros isn't sure how effective it could be: "I'm not sure you can regulate when we're talking about an entire nation of 300 million people and this behavior becomes viral." If anything needs to be regulated, it's the Federal Reserve's credit creation powers, which give legs to frenzies like the housing bubble, but in his interview with the *New York Times* Cisneros followed the rules: the Fed was never mentioned.

Andrew Cuomo, who also served as HUD secretary under Bill Clinton, spoke with delight after a victorious "discrimination" settlement with AccuBanc Mortgage that forced it to make loans on what the secretary admitted was an "affirmative action" basis. The institution would "take a greater risk on these mortgages, yes . . . give families mortgages who they would not have given otherwise, yes; they would not have qualified but for this affirmative action on the part of the bank, yes. . . . Lending that amount [\$2.1 billion] in mortgages which will be a higher risk, and I'm sure there will be a higher default rate on those mortgages than on the rest of the portfolio." So Secretary Cuomo was comfortable with forcing a bank to expose itself to more defaults, and isn't that what matters?

Liberals have argued that unscrupulous lenders dishonestly forced subprime mortgages with unfavorable or complicated terms on helpless and uneducated borrowers, and conservatives have argued that political pressure forced banks to make more of such loans. There is indeed some anecdotal evidence for the liberals' case, as we saw in the case of one of the people they themselves admire, Henry Cisneros. The conservatives have a strong case: left-wing groups like ACORN blocked drive-up lanes and made business impossible for banks until they surrendered to demands that they make billions in loans they wouldn't otherwise have made. This private intimidation, coupled with a campaign to lower lending standards that pervaded all levels of government, helped to steer so much of the new money the Fed was creating (see below) into the housing market, thereby feeding the housing bubble.

Culprit 3: The government's artificial stimulus to speculation

But in discussions of the mortgage meltdown there may in fact have been too much emphasis on subprime loans. Although the driving force behind abandoning traditional lending standards was the federal government's political goal of increasing homeownership, particularly among preferred minority groups, lending innovations like 100 percent loans (mortgages with no down payments) became institutionalized features of the industry, particularly when the Fed had made banks flush with reserves to lend. The push for relaxed lending standards for low- and middle-income borrowers was so pervasive and systematic, persisting for a full decade, that it is no surprise that it should have spilled over into the standards for higher-income borrowers as well. "Once this sloppy thinking had taken hold," writes Liebowitz, "it is naïve to believe that this decade-long attack on traditional underwriting standards would not also lead to more relaxed standards for higher-income borrowers as well. When everyone cheers for relaxed underwriting standards, the relaxation is not likely to be kept in narrow confines."[9] Not only were these easier mortgage terms available to speculators, but the surge in demand for housing caused by the much easier access to financing also led to increases in home prices that had the unintended effect of enticing speculators into the market in the first place. (A much more significant factor in raising home prices was the artificially low interest rates brought about by the Fed, as we'll see.)

It turns out that large increases in foreclosures occurred at the same time in both subprime and prime loans. Thus the subprime loan problem did not, as the headlines sometimes suggested, somehow infect the prime loan market. In fact, from 2006 through 2007, the increase in foreclosures started was much higher in the case of prime loans than in subprime loans. There were still more foreclosures in the subprime market in terms of absolute numbers, but that has always been the case, and that is why subprime loans carry higher interest rates.

Foreclosures primarily came about not because of subprime mortgages, but because of adjustable-rate mortgages—the ones Alan Greenspan had once urged people to use—whether prime or subprime. Adjustable-rate mortgages begin with what is called a teaser rate, a low interest rate that makes these mortgages initially attractive. After a set number of years the rate adjusts according to various economic indices. Sometimes the buyer will find himself with a higher interest rate and sometimes with a lower one. The adjustable-rate mortgage can perform a useful function in a climate of volatile interest rates, when neither borrower nor lender quite knows what the future will hold. Lenders are more likely to extend loans in such turbulent times if some of the risk can be shared with the borrower.

It turns out that there was a larger percentage increase in adjustable-rate *prime* mortgages than there was in subprime mortgages, where all the trouble was said to be. This, too, explodes the myth that the mortgage crisis came about because of unscrupulous lenders preying on vulnerable people who for whatever reason couldn't understand the mortgage terms they were agreeing to. If that were the case, how did prime adjustable-rate borrowers get more bamboozled than subprime borrowers?

The explanation for the rise in foreclosures that makes sense of the available data involves people who bought houses on a speculative basis, betting that their prices would continue to increase. This category includes people who "flipped" houses, meaning they made various improvements to houses and then sought to resell them at a high profit. It also includes people who expected to make a profit by buying a house, waiting a short period of time, and reselling for a profit based on the house's appreciation. In recent years speculative home buying has been estimated at about one-quarter of all home purchases. Both kinds of speculators would be attracted to the adjustable-rate mortgage, since they intend to unload their houses well before the teaser rate expires.

When housing prices started falling just a little bit (only 1.4 percent in six months starting in late 2006), foreclosures skyrocketed. Already at a record high, foreclosure starts shot dramatically upward, increasing by 43 percent over that span. It is likely that this sudden and seemingly disproportionate rise in foreclosures primarily involved homeowners who had used flexible, no-money-down mortgages to purchase homes planning to resell them at a profit. With housing prices no longer on the rise and the prospect of profit dwindling, many of these borrowers may simply have walked away. Not having made any down payment made walking away all the easier.[10]

This sudden collapse points to another culprit: the private agencies whose job it was to rate the creditworthiness of these mortgages. Why did the ratings agencies do such a poor job in assessing the risk factor in these mortgages? It could be argued that at a time when housing prices were consistently rising thanks to the Fed's cheap credit policy, these mortgages were performing well, and the ratings agencies therefore made the superficial decision to rate them highly. Another suggested explanation is that the agencies knew which way the wind was blowing, with every federal agency having even the slightest connection to housing pushing various homeownership initiatives that involved lowered lending standards.[11] According to economist Art Carden, "SEC regulations hung over the rating agencies like the sword of Damocles, and the raters didn't want to attract undue regulatory attention by opposing a politically popular initiative."[12]

The handful of approved ratings agencies, moreover, are actually an SEC-created cartel protected from competition by regulatory barriers. "Given that government-approved rating agencies were protected from free competition," writes Liebowitz, "it might be objected that these agencies would not want to create political waves by rocking the mortgage boat, endangering a potential loss of their protected profits."[13]

The cartel of ratings agencies deserves all the blame it has received. At the same time, as we'll see, the Federal Reserve's interventions into the economy distort economic indicators and make it harder for everyone, ratings agencies included, to perceive the true state of the economy. (That's culprit 5.)

Culprit 4: The "pro-ownership" tax code

Government, at the federal, state, and local level, developed hundreds of little programs intended to encourage more people to buy homes, thereby channeling more artificial demand into the housing sector. Developers constantly get handouts, free land, new roads, and tax privileges to build homes, even if—as is happening in far-out suburbs these days— nobody wants to buy them.

The tax code is the most obvious example. The federal government takes anywhere up to 35 percent of a worker's income (in addition to Social Security and Medicare taxes) unless he engages in certain activities. Invest in the stock market through an IRA or 401(k) and you can shield some money from the tax man. Pay premiums to a health insurance company through your employer, and you can deduct that money. The biggest deduction for most families is the home mortgage interest deduction. Renters and people who buy a home outright without taking out a mortgage don't get to write off their housing costs come tax day. Government introduces strong incentives to buy instead of rent—and to borrow heavily in order to buy.

There are countless little provisions like this. First-time homebuyers in Washington, D.C., for instance, receive a $5,000 tax credit. More significant is the special treatment accorded to a home as an investment. If you buy $500,000 in stock, or buy a business worth that much, and sell it ten years later for $1 million, you'll pay capital gains taxes (15 percent in 2008). Thanks to a 1997 law, if a couple bought a house for $500,000 and sold it for $1 million, they pay no capital gains taxes.

This is not to suggest that any of these tax breaks are undesirable or should be repealed; a "tax break" is an oasis of freedom to be broadened, not a loophole to be closed. Instead, they should be extended to as many other kinds of purchases as possible, in order not to provide artificial stimulus to any one sector of the economy.

Culprit 5: The Federal Reserve and artificially cheap credit

As true and important as all this is, though, these factors by themselves cannot account for the sheer scope of the housing bubble and the depth of the crash. To understand the housing boom and bust, we need to understand why business cycles occur. While conventional wisdom tells us that these booms and busts *just happen*, that conclusion lets government and its central bank off the hook.

Austrian economics, which we'll discuss in more depth in chapter 4, explains how business cycles occur—specifically, how government tinkering with the supply of money and credit starts the economy on an unsustainable boom that has to end in a bust.

When the Federal Reserve pushes down interest rates by increasing the money supply, it encourages a boom in the production of relatively longer-term projects: raw materials, construction, and capital goods in general. The boom in construction and real estate this past decade, made possible by these low interest rates, is a good example. Unlike the production that genuine consumer demand stimulates, though, the Fed's artificial stimulus is not in line with real consumer preferences or the current state of the economy's pool of savings. It draws resources away from projects that cater to real consumer demand, and it encourages more and different kinds of projects to be undertaken than the economy can sustain. The necessary resources to complete all these projects profitably do not exist. Neither the saved resources to complete them, nor the consumer base to purchase the finished products, exist in sufficient volume. Not enough people want or can afford half-million-dollar homes. The prices these homes can fetch are far lower than initially anticipated. The bust comes.

The Fed—whose mechanics will likewise be explained in a later chapter—started the boom by increasing the money supply through the banking system with the aim and the effect of lowering interest rates. In the wake of September 11, which came just over a year after the dot-com bust, then Fed chairman Alan Greenspan sought to reignite the economy through a series of rate cuts, culminating in the extraordinary decision to lower the target federal funds rate (the rate at which banks lend to one another overnight, and which usually drives other interest rates) to 1 percent for a full year, from June 2003 until June 2004. In order to bring about this result, the supply of money was increased dramatically during those years, with more dollars being created between 2000 and 2007 than in the rest of the republic's history.

This new money and credit overwhelmingly found its way into the housing market, where artificially lax lending standards made excessive home purchases and speculation in homes seem to many Americans like good financial moves. The Fed also encouraged the GSEs—Fannie Mae, Ginnie Mae, and Freddie Mac—and the Federal Housing Administration to borrow and lend at levels never before seen. So the already existing campaign to lower lending standards, along with the monopoly privileges enjoyed by the quasi-governmental agencies Fannie Mae and Freddie Mac, played a role in channeling into the housing market the new money the Fed was creating. But it was the Fed, ultimately, that made the artificial boom in housing possible in the first place, and it was all the new money it created that gave the biggest stimulus to the unnatural rise in housing prices.

Although speculators are one of the groups the political and media establishments teach us to loathe, there is nothing wrong with speculation in and of itself. In a truly free market, speculation—whether in real estate, commodities, or stocks—performs an important social function, making the economy more efficient by speeding the pace at which prices adjust to coordinate supply and demand. But an easy-money policy lures increasingly reckless or ill-prepared investors into the game, and misleads people into thinking a particular investment strategy is a no-lose proposition. Cheap money draws people into speculation who do not belong there, who know little about the market involved, and who see in it an irresistible get-rich-quick scheme.

And in fact, even without the added incentives introduced by new laws and regulations, an easier monetary policy by the Fed in and of itself encourages the lowering of lending standards. When banks lend out the new money created by the Fed, they necessarily lend it to people whom the banks had previously deemed unworthy. It's like the situation a basketball team would face if it added two new roster spots—those spots would go to players who would otherwise have been cut.[14] In an atmosphere of rising prices and general prosperity, it also becomes difficult to distinguish between sound projects and bubble projects—that is, between projects that would make good economic sense during normal times, and projects that can survive only if credit remains artificially cheap.

Phenomena like these are nothing new; observers have commented on them throughout American history. In the credit-induced boom from 1914 through 1920, for instance, the same excessive optimism, the same willingness to take on risk, the same artificial stimulus to speculation were all evident. According to Fred Garlock, writing about the situation in Iowa for the *Journal of Land & Public Utility Economics* in 1926, "caution was thrown to the wind by both bankers and their customers, speculation became rife, an enormous burden of debt was contracted, and economy was lost in a swirl of extravagance." Garlock explains how it works:

Rising prices affected both banks and their customers with an optimism which swept aside the conservative standards of experience and promoted extravagance and speculation. Whatever the customers purchased, whether merchandise or land, they were able to sell at an extraordinary profit; whatever was produced on their farms brought unusual returns. Some few persons, uncertain of what disposition should be made of the unexpected harvest, began reducing their fixed indebtedness. It was not long, however, until the continuously rising prices, the encouragement of the bankers, and the methods used by the government in selling war securities, had convinced the majority that debt was a blessing in disguise, as it became progressively easier to liquidate and offered a means of extending profit-making activities. Under the urge of these influences, industry expanded and thrived, promoters of all types came into their own, and thrift gave way to extravagance. Bankers found their accustomed standards of credit analysis growing obsolete, for values increased automatically with the passing of time. Hence it was that, as the speculative fever gained a foothold and grew and the demands for bank funds enlarged, credit was extended to all manner of persons on—or without—all kinds of security, excess lines became commonplace, customers' notes given to promoters of questionable and fraudulent enterprises were discounted for rich rewards, and large sums were advanced to land speculators. Borrowing for the purpose of relending became an established practice. Time and time again the banks were saved from the effects of their ill-advised acts by the continuous growth of deposits.[15]

This scenario should sound familiar. The same kind of real estate frenzy is evident throughout the history of American business cycles (which is also the history of artificial bank credit expansion) beginning with the Panic of 1819, and they could just as easily be drawn from news reports in 2008 and 2009.

Is "more regulation" the answer?

Financial "deregulation" has often been blamed for the economic meltdown, with then Senator Barack Obama late in the 2008 campaign season ceaselessly condemning the Bush administration's alleged drive to "strip away regulation." We'll have more to say about financial deregulation in the next chapter, but with regard to the housing market, the point is that lenders were doing *exactly what the federal government and its central bank wanted them to do*. Saying that more government oversight was needed misses the point. More and riskier loans are what the government wanted. Fashionable opinion everywhere, especially throughout the government sector, cheered as traditional lending practices were abandoned and riskier ones adopted—why, the American dream is being extended to more and more people!

And it wasn't just the Democrats—not by a long shot. In 2004 George W. Bush urged the Federal Housing Administration to lift the down-payment requirement altogether for 150,000 new homeowners. He declared, "To build an ownership society, we'll help even more Americans to buy homes. Some families are more than able to pay a mortgage but just don't have the savings to put money down."[16] The down payment, which had traditionally served to minimize defaults, was being swept aside by the president himself, and thus the trend away from traditional lending standards received a presidential imprimatur.

We are supposed to place our hopes in regulators who would have to be courageous enough to stand up against the entire political, academic, and media establishments? What regulator would have done anything differently, or dared to tell the regime something other than what it obviously wanted to hear?

People in high places, whose exalted offices lent an undeserved air of authority to what they said, assured everyone of the fundamental soundness of the system. Ben Bernanke himself assured the country that regulators investigating the mortgage market had found a smoothly functioning system and no cause for alarm. "Our examiners tell us that lending standards are generally sound and are not comparable to the standards that contributed to broad problems in the banking industry two decades ago. In particular, real estate appraisal practices have improved."[17] In 2004, two Fed economists published a study arguing there was no housing bubble.[18] Former Fed chairman Alan Greenspan actually encouraged borrowers to use adjustable-rate mortgages, which have since begun to reset at interest-rate levels that mean certain default for an ever-increasing number of homeowners. In 2003, Greenspan said rising housing prices did not amount to a bubble, though he did not expect them to continue to rise quite so fast. "The notion of a bubble bursting and a whole price level coming down seems to me as far as a nationwide phenomenon really quite unlikely," Greenspan told a Senate committee.[19] Apart from the economists of the Austrian School and a few others, who consistently pointed to the housing bubble and the damage it would inflict when it inevitably burst, few and far between were the voices of caution and sanity. Few could imagine that the entire real estate sector could experience a decline all at once, an idea that ran directly counter to the conventional wisdom that real estate was local and not characterized by national swings.

Some of the major financial institutions proceeded on the assumption that the housing boom was based on real factors and was not a mere bubble. These firms' behavior appeared risky only if the housing boom *was* a bubble. But the Fed's own economists denied that the housing boom was a bubble. What makes anyone so sure that a regulator would have seen the risk involved in these firms' bet that the housing boom was based on real factors and was not a bubble?

Even if some miraculous means were available by which regulators, given the task of overseeing the books of major financial institutions, could eliminate all major risk and see the economic picture more clearly than those whose own financial well-being actually depended on the outcome, we would still be dealing with a symptom, albeit a significant one, rather than with the cause. As long as the Fed can create as much money as it wants and push interest rates down to destructively low levels, bubble activity—that is, wealth-destroying activity that seems profitable only because the Fed has kept interest rates artificially low—will occur *somewhere*. If it wasn't the mortgage markets and the financial industry that became distorted, it would have been something else.

Culprit 6: The "too Big to Fail" mentality

Certain actors in financial markets have been able to operate in the confidence that they, and the system as a whole, will not be allowed to fail, and that in one way or another the American population will absorb the losses. Alan Greenspan solidified a reputation for himself among investors as Mr. Bailout, what with his 1994 bailout of the Mexican peso, the special rate cuts meant to ease the distress of the Long Term Capital Management hedge fund, and the flooding of the banking system with fresh reserves in the wake of September 11, among numerous other examples. This, says economist Antony Mueller, is the philosophy (if it can be called that) that guided the Greenspan Fed from its inception in 1987:

> Since Alan Greenspan took office, financial markets in the U.S. have operated under a quasi-official charter, which says that the central bank will protect its major actors from the risk of bankruptcy. Consequently, the reasoning emerged that when you succeed, you will earn high profits and market share, and if you should fail, the authorities will save you anyway.... When monetary authorities repeatedly act to ward off economic downturns and continue to feed the markets with fresh liquidity, the belief in an eternal boom becomes more widespread each time, and economic activity becomes more intensive. With the continuation of

such a boom, prudence diminishes, and new types of entrepreneurs appear.[20]

Analysts have sometimes called this the "Greenspan put,"* what the *Financial Times* describes as the view that "when markets unravel, count on the Federal Reserve and its chairman Alan Greenspan (eventually) to come to the rescue." The *Times* reported in 2000, in the wake of the dot-com boom, an increasing concern that the Greenspan put was injecting into the economy "a destructive tendency toward excessively risky investment supported by hopes that the Fed will help if things go bad." "All the insane dot-com investment we've seen, all this destruction of capital, all the crazy excesses of the past few years wouldn't have happened without the easy credit accommodated by the Fed," added financial consultant Michael Belkin.[21]

Try letting a few major firms—yes, even in the financial sector, where we superstitiously believe no failures can be allowed—actually go bankrupt for a change. Make perfectly clear once and for all that there will be no bailouts, no looting of the public, on behalf of any firm, period. That would do more to jolt the financial sector into being sensible and cautious instead of reckless and irresponsible than all the regulatory tinkering in the world.

The future

Congress, the Bush administration, and the Obama administration have been considering just about every policy under the sun—except allowing the market to set housing prices where they obviously belong.

In November 2008, Fannie and Freddie announced that they would take emergency action to help distressed homeowners avoid foreclosure.

---

*A "put option," or a "put," gives a buyer the right to sell an asset at a given price. The term "Greenspan put" derives from this usage. The suggestion is that, just as in a traditional put, the figurative Greenspan put places a floor beneath asset prices, since Greenspan and the Fed will prop up troubled asset classes if necessary.

Homeowners are eligible for the assistance—which involves reductions in principal owed, lower interest rates, and a longer payoff term—if they are at least 90 days delinquent on their mortgage payments and have high debt-to-income ratios, and their mortgages are owned or guaranteed by Fannie or Freddie. They must also owe at least 90 percent of their home's value. So if you bought more house than you could afford, if you took out home equity loans to purchase consumption goods, and if you're missing your payments, you get special consideration. In fact, under the program, people who bought luxury cars with the proceeds from refinancing their homes get to keep those things, and are not expected to sell them in order to pay their mortgages.

If you behaved responsibly and bought a smaller house than you could afford, on the other hand, and didn't treat your house as a giant ATM, you get no special consideration. In fact, you indirectly subsidize the foolish and improvident.

Under this program, Fannie and Freddie will reduce monthly mortgage payments to as low as 38 percent of household income. Any principal reductions will be payable as a lump sum at the end of the mortgage period, or at the time the house is sold. Thus the program is intended both to keep people from being foreclosed on *and* to keep them from selling their homes. It indirectly props up home prices by keeping such dwellings off the market.

In light of this offer, why wouldn't people whose mortgage loans are backed by Fannie and Freddie just stop making their mortgage payments altogether, confident that the result will be a friendly telephone call offering them lower rates and principal, and lower monthly payments? If the home is occupied by a married couple, one of the two individuals could also stop working, in order to lower household income so that the new mortgage payment, calculated in terms of household income, will be all the easier to make. Then the out-of-work spouse could return to work. Or a homeowner could take a minimum-wage job, or ask for a temporary pay cut at his current job, in order to get a mortgage payment of 38 percent of his lower income. One's credit rating would suffer if he

defaulted in order to get a lower rate, but that's a trade-off some homeowners are doubtless willing to make, especially since delinquency causes
less damage to a credit report than foreclosure.

In December, a proposal was discussed whereby the Treasury would
take various measures to reduce mortgage rates to 4.5 percent in order
to make housing more affordable. As usual, we are promised that artificially low interest rates will solve our problems, and that the fact of
scarcity can be wished away by government action. Of course, just letting home prices fall would make housing more affordable, and would
make it possible for people to purchase homes *without* getting themselves
so deep into debt, but this option is never even considered. The government is determined to press forward in its war on reality and against natural market valuations of homes.

And as usual, more of what caused the problem in the first place has
been put forth as the solution. Alan Greenspan lowered interest rates to
1 percent for a full year, thereby intensifying the housing bubble and the
pain that its inevitable burst would cause. As of late 2008, Fed chairman
Ben Bernanke was aiming to bring interest rates down to just about zero.
We are in for more resource misallocation and a more intense bust in the
future. Greenspan tried to inflate his way out of a recession in 2000 and
2001, and the result was the worse one we face now. By trying to hold
off this one, the Fed promises us a future that is worse still.

Economist Gerald O'Driscoll, a former senior Fed official, compares
the Fed to "an arsonist watching a fire he set, expressing amazement at
how such an event could have happened."[22] Bernanke can pretend the
Fed had nothing to do with the crisis, and can even repeat the exact policies that brought us to where we are, since no one will call him on it.
Most Americans, unfortunately, don't know the first thing about the Fed,
the quacks who operate it, or the Austrian theory of the business cycle.
And most of Bernanke's vocal critics, even the ones who are supposed to
be the experts, condemn him only for not lowering rates fast enough.

As we'll see in chapter 4, this is *the very worst policy* to adopt. And
as we'll see by the end of this book, policies that might keep recessions

short and swift are inevitably passed over in favor of proposals that will make Americans poorer and keep the hard times going.

We are really in for it.

CHAPTER 3

THE GREAT WALL STREET BAILOUT

Treasury secretary Henry Paulson, speaking of the global economy in March 2007, said "it's as strong as I've seen it in my business career."[1] "Our financial institutions are strong," he added in March 2008. "Our banks are strong. They're going to be strong for many, many years."[2]

Federal Reserve chairman Ben Bernanke echoed this sentiment. In May 2007, as the housing collapse began to hit our economy, Bernanke said, "We do not expect significant spillovers from the subprime market to the rest of the economy or to the financial system."[3]

But things did spill over. By mid-March 2008, Wall Street investment bank Bear Stearns was collapsing. Rather than let it collapse, the Fed jumped in and bailed it out by "lending" money to investment bank JP Morgan, with Bear Stearns' worthless mortgage-backed securities as collateral. The Federal Reserve, without any vote in Congress, simply bought Bear Stearns and handed it to JP Morgan. Why? The "systemic risk" that a Bear Stearns disappearance would allegedly cause. This "strong" economy was being treated very gingerly indeed.

In August 2008, Paulson and Bernanke assured the country that other than perhaps another bailout—this one for Fannie and Freddie—the fundamentals of the economy were sound.[4]

Don't panic. Don't stop investing. Don't stop borrowing to buy homes. Spend like you're Paris Hilton. Everything is just fine.

You would think that anyone who fed the public such lines through the first eight months of 2008 would have lost all credibility—and probably his job. But not only did Bernanke and Paulson retain their positions as the stock market melted down in September, but these men, who were proven so wrong in their assessment of the situation, also demanded unprecedented new powers to fix it.

The bailouts begin

While everything had been just fine only moments before, by September radical measures were suddenly necessary to stave off a financial calamity of historic proportions. On September 7, Secretary Paulson announced that the U.S. government would take over Fannie Mae and Freddie Mac, the institutions that had been packaging 75 percent of all American mortgage loans. Fannie and Freddie held $5 trillion in mortgage liabilities, and no one knew what fraction of that sum was in danger of default. The arrangement was called "conservatorship," but everyone knew it was simple *nationalization*: the direct government takeover of a private (or quasi-private, as in this case) institution.

Just like that, the secretary of the Treasury had taken over most of the American mortgage market. Neither Congress nor anyone else was consulted. Paulson suggested that taxpayers might actually gain from the transaction, since the federal government placed itself ahead of the common shareholders to receive whatever profits these giants might post in the future. More likely are at least hundreds of billions in losses, to be picked up by the taxpayer. The *New York Times* lived up to its normal level of sycophancy, calling this taxpayer guarantee of dubious assets a "reasonable and reassuring move." (By November, Fannie was reporting a $29 billion third-quarter loss, and warning that by the end of the year its net worth could be negative.)

Things began unraveling quickly. The following week the Fed orchestrated Bank of America's purchase of Merrill Lynch. Shortly beforehand, Paulson had lined up ten financial institutions to work out a bailout for Lehman Brothers. Merrill Lynch was one of those ten. "Paulson was so out of the loop," wrote one observer, "that he did not realize that not only could Merrill Lynch not come up with $7 billion as its share of the proposed bailout [of Lehman], it would cease to exist as a separate institution before the day was over."[5]

Lehman Brothers was ultimately allowed to go bankrupt. Paulson explained at the time that there would be no wave of bailouts. He did not want to encourage moral hazard. *Moral hazard* is the increased likelihood of risky behavior when the acting party believes that any costs of his behavior will be borne not by himself alone but by a large pool of people—as when a firm behaves recklessly because it expects to be bailed out with other people's resources. "Moral hazard is something I don't take lightly," he said.[6]

The next day an $85 billion bailout of insurance giant AIG was announced.

AIG found itself in trouble not so much because it was heavily invested in mortgage-backed securities but because it had issued so many credit default swaps on them—in effect insurance policies against defaults. The consequences of the bursting housing bubble for mortgage-backed securities were grim. With housing values going down, interest rates going up on adjustable-rate mortgages, and more and more people either upside-down in their mortgages (owing more than their houses were worth) or about to be hit with dramatically higher monthly payments, foreclosures were inevitable. The securities into which these mortgages had been bundled soon tumbled in value. Their plummeting values, in turn, amounted to a crisis for AIG.

The Fed's bailout of AIG was, in the words of the *New York Times*, "the most radical intervention in private business in the central bank's history."[7] The Fed would lend AIG $85 billion in exchange for 80 percent of the company. Congress, as usual, was not consulted. Meanwhile, social studies teachers across the country continued to report for work to detail how a bill becomes a law, how the will of the people is the guiding principle of the U.S. government, and how the public good motivates their government officials.

By November, AIG needed another $40 billion.

Washington had become a beggar's alley for corporations, and taxpayers had become milk cows.

Too big to fail?

AIG, Fannie and Freddie, the Big Three automakers (which jumped on the gravy train when they saw the money flowing), and others sure to come are said to be "too big to fail"—that is, too big for the public to let fail. The argument is that the failure of a large firm that is significantly connected to other firms could send ripple effects throughout the economy, and a great many other firms could wind up toppling as well.

But there is an alternative way to think about large-scale failures. If a single company has four profitable activities and two unprofitable ones, discontinuing the unprofitable activities is good for that company. Instead of squandering resources in areas that poorly satisfy consumer demand, the company can reallocate those previously invested resources toward its four profitable activities. The company is *healthier* for having sloughed off its parasitic sectors, and can now expand with renewed vigor.

What is true for this single company is no less true for the aggregate of wealth producers that constitute the whole economy: discontinuing activities that destroy wealth and drain resources away from healthy, competent firms is a step *forward* for the economy.

In that sense, these firms we're told are too big to fail are in fact *too big to be kept alive*. The longer they are kept on life support, the more they drain capital and resources away from fundamentally sound firms that could put those resources to much more productive use from consumers' point of view.[8] Keeping such firms alive via government bailouts discourages rather than encourages capital formation and economic recovery.

The fate of Lehman Brothers is a good example of what happens to a firm that is allowed to fail, and what happens to the rest of the economy when a gigantic firm goes under. With assets totaling $639 billion and some 26,000 employees, Lehman could have made a good argument that it was too big to fail. In fact, though, it wasn't. What was good and worth preserving in Lehman found other homes at the hands of other owners when it went under in September 2008; what was not worth preserving disappeared. That is what happens when bankruptcy is declared. The earth did not break free of its orbit and go tumbling toward the sun.

Washington Mutual, or WaMu, was the largest American savings and loan bank, and it had to liquidate in September 2008. JP Morgan Chase bought some of its good assets. Life went on.

The Mother Of All Bailouts

By the end of September 2008, the Bush administration had decided that these one-off bailouts weren't doing the trick. Something bigger was needed. Much bigger.

Secretary Paulson and Fed chairman Bernanke presented Americans with a comprehensive bailout package for the financial sector that Respectable Opinion urged them to accept. They were told all kinds of horror stories of what would happen to them if they failed to do as their betters told them: the decimation of their retirement plans, the collapse of housing prices, the inability of small businesses to make payroll (as if a healthy small business borrows to make payroll), and on and on. The bailout had to be passed right away. Anyone opposing or even calling for delay in passing this bill was an ideologue and a fool. There was no time even to read what eventually became a 442-page bill. There was certainly no time for debate. And what was there to debate? *Credit is freezing up!*

In fact, credit continued to be available to the creditworthy—a sensible principle that if observed in recent years might have saved us much grief—albeit with a higher risk premium at a time of such uncertainty. But we should *want* credit to freeze up during a recession, particularly in a case like the present one, in which so many unanswered questions hover over so many sectors. Excessive, imprudent lending and credit creation led to the economy's depressed condition in the first place by misallocating so much capital into unprofitable and even absurd lines of production. The economy needs time to restructure itself, for market participants to sort out which investments are sound and which are squandering capital, and for asset prices to be brought back into line with reality, in order for rational economic calculation to proceed once again. Banks should do exactly what they appear to be doing: restoring sane and sensible lending standards and scrutinizing loan applications more carefully.

The bailout bill—excuse me, the Emergency Economic Stabilization Act of 2008—authorized the Treasury to purchase $700 billion in assets "at any one time." That of course means it could buy that much in assets, sell them (almost inevitably) at a loss, then buy $700 billion more, and do so again and again. Declan McCullagh of CBS News warned that under the law a bank could "buy $100 billion of bad debt—perhaps in the form of subprime mortgages that are becoming quickly worthless— declare bankruptcy, and sell it to the Treasury Department for $200 billion."[9] The point of these purchases was to take bad assets off the hands of financial institutions in order to reduce the uncertainty and hesitation that was said to be disrupting interbank lending (with relatively healthy institutions hesitant to lend to banks they thought might be holding bad assets) and get interbank lending flowing more vigorously again. The taxpayer would thus be on the hook for the bad assets instead. We also read that "troubled assets are not limited to mortgage-related assets but could include auto loans, credit card debt, student loans or any other paper related to commercial loans."

Under the Troubled Assets Relief Program, the Treasury can seize any financial institution's asset at whatever price it dictates. The institution has no legal recourse, according to Section 119, which reads: "No action or claims may be brought against the Secretary by any person that divests its assets with respect to its participation in a program under this Act, except as provided in paragraph (1), other than as expressly provided in a written contract with the Secretary." It's like eminent domain for financial assets. If Treasury wants it, and your bank has it, Treasury can take it for whatever price it wants. Of course, for now, big financial institutions favor such a program—it means selling worthless stuff to the government. The Treasury also acquires the power to "guarantee" home mortgages at taxpayer expense and take measures to reduce foreclosures, including eliminating a "reasonable" amount of an individual's mortgage debt.

There was quite a sound and persuasive argument against the bailout, but all the same, American citizens were scolded by their betters for not accepting with alacrity the pronouncements of Paulson and Bernanke. David Brooks, one of the alleged conservatives at the *New York Times*, carried on the *Times*'s streak of being wrong on everything by denouncing those who resisted as "the authors of this revolt of the nihilists. They showed the world how much they detest their own leaders and the collected expertise of the Treasury and Fed."[10] Brooks evidently has in mind the "collected expertise" of people who for years had been ludicrously mistaken in their assessments of the economy, whose statements and proposals changed from week to week, and who obviously hadn't the slightest idea what was happening. Not to take direction from such people is, according to Brooks, an indication of nihilism, with a complete reversion to barbarism surely not far behind.

Short-selling is unpatriotic

The federal government's approach to the financial crisis included a ban on short-selling the stocks of 799 specific firms. Short-selling is a strategy investors pursue when they expect a company's share price to fall. If someone expects a stock to increase in value, he buys shares of that stock. If he expects it to decline in value, he can short the stock.

Anticipating a fall in the share price of a particular company, he borrows some quantity of that company's stock, sells it at the current (and in his estimation, overvalued) price, and then, when the price falls, he purchases the same quantity of shares at the lower price to return to the stockholder from whom he borrowed them. The short-seller pockets the difference.

To keep matters simple, suppose you borrow one share of a company whose stock price is $100. You then sell that share for the going price of $100. Two weeks later the share price falls to $80. At that point you buy a share to return to the person you borrowed from in the first place (a person who had not intended to sell those shares in the first place). You keep the difference—in this case, $20.

Bans on short-selling have perverse effects, exactly contrary to the purpose for which they are proposed. If investors are to place their money somewhere, they need to know which positions are sound and which unsound. If speculators massively short certain companies, the remaining companies are implicitly given a clean bill of health. Investors can thereby make a safer, more informed decision about where to put their money. Without this information, investors will be even more cautious, and those outlets that have been the soundest and most responsible with their money will find it all the more difficult to raise funds.[11]

Regulators tend to be highly critical of short-selling. And no wonder: short-sellers often show up the failures of regulators. It is regulators, after all, who are supposed to ferret out fraud, dubious accounting practices, and whatever else might tend to make a firm's profitability seem greater than it really is. Short-sellers, particularly those with inside knowledge, do the work that regulators are supposed to do, and often call attention to questionable firms before regulators themselves do, if indeed regulators ever do at all.

This is precisely what happened with Enron in late 2001. The Securities and Exchange Commission (SEC) unfailingly gave Enron the stamp of approval, even as the company's accounting and deal-making became curiouser and curiouser. It was a short-seller, namely James Chanos, who peered into Enron's finances and saw a rotting corpse. Chanos shorted the stock and blew the whistle. When everyone else turned around and studied Enron, they all saw it for what it was—a fraud. It was the short-seller who had the motivation and the smarts to seek out such an over-valued fraud.

So short-sellers are a rebuke to the regulatory apparatus, which by its very existence lulls investors into a false sense of security about the health and practices of a firm—surely the regulators would tell me if something were wrong!—and a reminder of just one of many forms of private regulation that would exist in the absence of the omniscient public servants who look after us now.[12]

Furthermore, without short-selling, the only people who would be able to communicate their belief that a stock was overpriced would be the current owners of a company's stock. But there is no reason to think that only those people would have useful information about the firm. That short-sellers are wrong sometimes is certainly true, but who isn't? People who buy stock and hold it also turn out, quite often, to be wrong. And even when they're right, that means that whoever sold them the stock initially was wrong (if he did so because he expected its price to fall).[13] Arguments against short-selling are, to put it mildly, without merit.

Bailout bonanza

The ban on short-selling was just one of a whole arsenal of bad ideas that were supposed to help the economy improve. In October 2008, the Federal Deposit Insurance Corporation (FDIC) increased the amount of each bank deposit it would insure from $100,000 to $250,000, a measure that is supposed to expire in December 2009. FDIC insurance allows people to deposit money at banks without considering the soundness of the bank's finances, because if the bank were to go under, the FDIC would cover their deposits.

So, at the very time that banks need to become more cautious and conservative, the federal government adds yet another layer of moral hazard to the equation, and at the same time lowers the incentive for scrutiny on the part of potential depositors. (The FDIC's assets suffice to cover about one half of one percent of all the deposits it insures, so in the case of a string of bank collapses, the federal government would have to resort to the printing press and massive inflation in order to make good on its so-called insurance.[14])

Some writers have proposed foreclosure holidays, in which for some period of time (60 days, say) no home foreclosures would be allowed. The predictable result would be to entice marginal borrowers, who with effort might have continued to make their payments, into not making them any longer, thereby exacerbating the problem. Lenders, observing this arbitrary interference with the rights of contract and with their ability to take possession of collateral, will simply extend less credit in the first place. At that point, the reduced availability of mortgage loans will be cited as further evidence of the free market's inadequate provision for the common man.

Is "deregulation" the problem?

While most attacks on "deregulation" lacked specifics and were merely knee-jerk responses by opponents of the market economy, those who argue that deregulation had nothing to do with the crisis are also missing an essential piece of the puzzle. Commercial bank deposits are *insured by the federal government* up to $100,000 (and, temporarily, up to $250,000). Any "deregulation" of the banking system that permits the banks to take greater risks while maintaining government (that is, taxpayer) insurance of their deposits is not genuine deregulation from a free-market point of view.

When the moral hazard of deposit insurance is combined with the "too big to fail" mentality, which will not allow large institutions to fail, the result (a conclusion compelled by common sense and bolstered by recent research) is that banks will take on considerably more risk than they would if they were subject to genuine market pressures.[15]

This is the context in which regulation and deregulation have to be considered: a system so far removed from the free market that innocent third parties are on the hook for private firms' foolish and risky decisions. In that context, is "deregulation" necessarily the best approach? Of course, *real* deregulation, which would abolish all monopoly privileges, establish free competition, eliminate the "too big to fail" presumption, and force banks to produce their depositors' money on demand or declare bankruptcy—in other words, treating banking just like every other industry—would be the most welcome outcome of all. But a mixture of liberalizing banks' risk-taking ability while maintaining a government guarantee may be the worst of both worlds.[16]

Recall the Savings and Loan crisis of the 1980s, in which the federal government came to the rescue of the failing S&Ls. That fiasco, too, was supposedly the result of "deregulation." But once again, "regulation" and "deregulation" are utterly beside the point. The point is that, as with Fannie and Freddie, and now the great investment banks, the taxpayer was on the hook for these institutions' bad decisions. That makes such institutions less cautious and more reckless than they would otherwise be, since they can spread out, or socialize, their risk across the broad expanse of the taxpaying public. "Deregulating" the S&Ls to allow them to make riskier investments—which was widely regarded from 1980 onward as a critical step to keep them from sinking—is "deregulation" in only the most perverse and unhelpful sense. Real deregulation would have cut the S&Ls' ties to the taxpayer entirely.

The problem, in short, is not "regulation" or the lack thereof. Once again, the problem is the system itself, a system that (as we'll see in later chapters) artificially encourages indebtedness, excessive leverage, and reckless money management in general. The money and banking system we have now, which is nearly as far removed from a genuine free market as it is possible to be, is so fragile and prone to instability that it's no wonder people call for more "regulation."

But why should we be satisfied to regulate a house of cards when we can take the much more sensible step of allowing the free market to establish a far sounder, less crisis-prone system in its place, a system needing no taxpayer bailouts and afflicted by no moral hazard? Shouting matches over regulation versus deregulation necessarily neglect this genuine free-market alternative.

In practice, moreover, calls for "more regulation" wind up suffocating the market in response to a handful of notorious wrongdoers. They are an anti-terrorism strategy that is always prepared for yesterday's terrorist—there will never be another shoe bomber aboard a commercial plane, but we sure are ready for him.

In the wake of the Enron scandal and the dot-com boom and bust, Congress passed Sarbanes-Oxley, a regulatory act that well-established firms came to welcome since they knew it would give them a competitive advantage against newcomers. They had no idea how much. The most recent estimated annual cost to implement it in a public corporation is $3.5 million.

"The closer you look at Sarbanes-Oxley," writes a critic, "the more you realize it is almost perfectly designed to crush new business creation.... [$3.5 million is] pocket change for a Fortune 500 company, [but] the entire annual profit of a newly public firm. Is it really any wonder that smart entrepreneurs look for a corporate sugar daddy instead of an IPO?" Add to that Regulation FD ("Fair Disclosure") and the new rules on stock option valuation, and the result is that "fewer new companies are going public; economic power is being concentrated in the hands of fewer companies; competition is reduced; new wealth is less widely distributed; the rich are getting richer; fewer talented people want to join entrepreneurial ventures; and corporate boards are getting stupider and more paranoid."[17] That could be why the biggest, most established firms typically seem to favor additional regulatory burdens. Expect to hear them joining the chorus today, solemnly informing us how sadly necessary additional regulation is.

So we have little reason to believe regulation will prevent the repeat of such excesses, and in retrospect there's no reason to think more regulation would have made our pain any less.

Overblown crisis

Even on its own terms, it is unclear that the desperate measures of the bailout were called for. Lending had not in fact evaporated. Business was still going on.

In October 2008 three economists for the Federal Reserve Bank of Minneapolis released a study showing that four major scare claims that had been advanced on behalf of the bailout were false. First, it was not true that bank lending across the board had declined sharply. Wall Street firms had trouble borrowing (except from the government), but not the rest of us. As of October 8, the data showed no decline in business and consumer loans. Second, interbank lending, which was being described as essentially nonexistent, was in fact "healthy" according to the data. Third, non-financial businesses showed no sharp decline in their ability to secure short-term loans (called "commercial paper"). Although commercial paper issued by financial institutions had declined, commercial paper issued by nonfinancial institutions showed essentially no change during the crisis. Interest rates on commercial paper rose for financial institutions, but not for everybody else (and even the rate for financial institutions was still considerably lower than it had been from 2006 through mid-2007). Finally, even if banks were lending less, that didn't spell doom for businesses hoping to borrow; the study found that about 80 percent of business borrowing took place outside the banking system.[18]

Celent, the financial services consultancy, released a report in December 2008 that corroborated this Fed study. Using the Fed's own figures, the report concluded that the alleged "credit crunch" was totally overblown: the amount of lending had been very high all throughout the crisis, including everything from consumer credit to interbank loans. The U.S. government, the report suggested, was falsely extrapolating from the difficulties of a number of large, high-profile institutions (especially commercial and investment banks and the automobile industry) to the more general conclusion that a credit freeze was afflicting the economy at large. "It is startling that many of Chairman Bernanke and Secretary Paulson's remarks are not supported or are flatly contradicted by the data provided by the very organizations they lead," the report said.[19]

Do *something!*

But the data on which these reports were based was ignored by Congress, the administration, and the media covering the mad rush to this massive bailout. There was just no time for alternative points of view, you see, or even to collect all the relevant information about what was happening. Our leaders didn't have the luxury of sober reflection at a time like this. They had to act.

If that sounds familiar, it's because this is what government always says whenever it's trying to get away with something.

So, under pressure from all quarters of respectable opinion, Congress took up the bailout. The Senate passed it almost unanimously. It had been a matter of genuine surprise days earlier when the House of Representatives, in the face of the scare tactics, the smears, the media consensus in support of dumb economics, managed to vote it down.

The script was predictable enough: when the stock market fell in the ensuing days, that was because the bailout hadn't passed the House. Soon enough, the House was brought back into the room to vote the right way. The bailout passed and was signed by the president on October 2. That day, the Dow Jones Industrial Average closed at 10,482. A week later, the Dow was well below 9,000, and it stayed below that mark for most of the rest of the year.

So the bailout didn't seem to save the economy after all, and in the ensuing weeks and months the ongoing bailout mania struck an increasingly skeptical American public as little more than a giant black hole for money and resources. Of course, had the bailout ultimately been defeated, the stock market's woes would have been blamed on the refusal of Congress to approve the bailout. There was no way for the market economy to win this rigged debate.

Even if the various provisions of the bailout would take time to implement, the knowledge that they *would* be implemented should have given Wall Street a boost, just as the knowledge that new supplies of oil will be available in the future puts downward pressure on prices in the present. (Little rallies here and there always occur during bear markets— the Dow reached historic highs during the early period of what we now call the Great Depression.)

Well, if it wasn't working, some observers suggested, it was because the authorities hadn't poured in quite enough money. But not only had the bailout package's promise of over $700 billion not been enough, but the $800 billion the Fed and the Treasury had directed into lesser bailouts for the previous half year had also failed to produce any results. All they had to show for themselves was a *Weekend at Bernie's* economy, with sunglasses and Hawaiian shirts on zombie companies supposed to give the impression of life and health.

Although the plan that the Bush administration had demanded *right now* lest we fall into another Great Depression involved purchasing bad assets from financial institutions, the Treasury, once given this authority, postponed that plan. Finally, they abandoned it altogether.

In other words, the people to whom we have entrusted a total of $8 trillion to lend or give away do not have the faintest idea what they are doing.

To the left of Hugo Chavez: Nationalizing the banks

In a statement on October 8, Secretary Paulson reminded Americans that the bailout package empowered the Treasury "to use up to $700 billion to inject capital into financial institutions, to purchase or insure mortgage assets, and to purchase any other troubled assets that the Treasury and the Federal Reserve deem necessary to promote financial market stability."[20] It was perhaps no coincidence that the Secretary listed these strategies in the order he did, since although the Treasury had previously emphasized the latter two, the newly favored strategy was now direct injections of "capital" into the banks.

Neel Kashkari, the former vice president of Goldman Sachs chosen by ex-Goldman Sachs CEO Henry Paulson as interim head of the Treasury Department's new Office of Financial Stability (what would a new government agency be without an Orwellian title?), explained several days later that the program would be "designed with attractive terms to encourage participation from *healthy institutions*."[21] The federal government would seek ownership stakes in banks, handing over $250 billion in exchange for shares of stock. Half the money would go to nine large institutions, including Citibank, Bank of America, and Goldman Sachs, and the other half would be divided among smaller institutions. According to the *New York Times*, Paulson told top bankers that "they would have to accept government investment for the good of the American financial system."[22]

Even Hugo Chavez, Venezuela's socialist president, found this a stunning move for a nominally market economy to take. "Bush is to the left of me now," he said. "Comrade Bush announced he will buy shares in private banks."[23]

So now Americans were expected to hand over their money, fall deeper into debt, or watch their currency's value deteriorate so that *healthy* institutions could receive injections of cash. (Remember, there's no time to debate any of this—these healthy institutions need money *now*!) Oh, and don't worry, we're told: government ownership of banks is only temporary. A valuable assurance indeed in light of our government's pristine track record of voluntarily relinquishing its emergency powers. (Speaking of which, the Fed's loan to AIG was justified on the basis of a previous emergency power granted during the Great Depression, over 70 years earlier.[24])

Government intervention in banking does not mean a more sensible, more responsible approach to lending will replace the wild risks of recent years. Wild risks will still be taken, except with the beneficiaries being selected more deliberately from among the ranks of politicians' friends and various favored constituencies. "Government ownership," warns Harvard's Jeffrey Miron, "means that political forces will determine who wins and who loses in the banking sector. The government, for example, will push banks to aid borrowers with poor credit histories, to subsidize politically connected industries, and to lend in the districts of powerful members of Congress."[25]

Whatever parties the government may pressure the banks to lend to, government officials want them lending to *someone*, right away. To the frustration of federal officials, the institutions that received these essentially involuntary infusions of government "capital" did not rush out and lend it. To a sensible person, that seems like a reasonable course of action: with the economy on its way down, banks have to be especially careful to ensure that any new borrowers are able to repay their loans. More to the point, the current crisis, having been caused by excessive and imprudent lending, is not going to be solved by still more politically motivated and artificially stimulated lending. That isn't how the government sees things, of course. White House press secretary Dana Perino lectured the misbehaving banks: "What we're trying to do is get banks to do what they are supposed to do, which is support the system that we have in America. And banks exist to lend money."[26] First the complaint had been that the banks were too reckless, and not careful and conservative enough. Now it was that the banks were being too careful.

Contradictions and reversals were everywhere by now, as terrified government officials ran around like chickens with their heads cut off, utterly in the dark regarding what to do or why the world refused to conform to what they had learned in the standard economics text. By mid-November, for instance, Secretary Paulson had all but abandoned the idea of purchasing toxic mortgage-based assets from financial institutions, prompting speculation either that this had never been the true intent of the bailout bill, or that Paulson was so confused about what was happening to the economy that he could scarcely decide on a course of action. The idea had never been a particularly good one. The federal government had argued that if it bought these mortgages and held them to maturity, it would earn their face value. Right now, the argument went, these mortgage-based assets were temporarily illiquid, but if government bought and held them they would fetch much higher prices in the long run than they could today. Overlooked in this rosy scenario was the likelihood of default on so many of these mortgages, which would never reach maturity since the payments would no longer be forthcoming.

And these assets were not nearly as illiquid as conventional wisdom held: there *were* buyers for them, but not at the unrealistic prices that some, including government, hoped for. In fact, as soon as Henry Paulson announced that the government would not be purchasing these bad assets after all, private hedge-fund manager John Paulson (no relation) indicated his intention to buy up some of these assets himself.[27] Government would have tried to keep housing prices propped up by acquiring these assets at prices no one else would have paid. But these assets were so numerous that to acquire enough of them to have a noticeable effect would have required the creation of so much new money that the effort would have destroyed the dollar.

For whatever reason, Secretary Paulson suddenly decided that this was not the way to spend the hundreds of billions of dollars he had asked for. Instead, it was now the consumer credit markets that needed to be propped up. "Illiquidity in this sector is raising the cost and reducing the availability of car loans, student loans and credit cards," Paulson warned.[28] Because if there's one thing Americans need more of, it's credit card offers. And the cruel fate of having to keep your car for an additional year or two instead of buying a new one—it's just too terrible to contemplate.

Should consumer credit actually become slightly more difficult to come by, full-fledged panic does not seem like the sensible response. The market would thereby be saying that Americans needed to start saving a little, instead of buying another plasma TV on credit. But our rulers cannot leave well enough alone. The very thought never occurs to them. If they weren't looting the general public to bail out some wealth destroyer they would hardly know what to do with themselves.

Scattershot bailouts

All these efforts were supposed to increase "confidence" in the system. But the course of action the Treasury and the Fed took and continue to take has been so erratic and extreme that the net effect seems to have been greater uncertainty. From day to day no one knows what will happen next, what new rules will be made, what sectors will be targeted for bailouts, and so on. Paulson's repeated changes of mind and strategy have left many market participants with the strong impression that the American authorities have no idea what they are doing—a realization that does not exactly boost investor confidence. This is one of the problems that dogged Franklin Roosevelt throughout the New Deal: his administration was so erratically interventionist that businessmen understandably held back from investing, unsure of what it might do next.[29]

Even before the bailout package proposed in September and the government purchase of bank stocks, the Fed had begun massive lending to banks in exchange for collateral of dubious value. These earlier bailouts had been going on since 2007 and intensified in 2008. Seeking creative new ways to pump additional money into the system, the Fed established the Term Auction Facility (TAF), the Term Securities Lending Facility (TSLF), and the Primary Dealer Credit Facility (PDCF). Hundreds of billions of dollars were made available to the financial system via these means. The PDCF in particular allows the Fed to make direct loans to investment banks through its discount window, an action it had not taken since the Great Depression. Investment banks could now receive loans in exchange for securities that were almost sure to lose value. Peter Boockvar, equity strategist for Miller Tabak, argued that these special arrangements and injections of money only intensified the underlying problems and diminished financial firms' sense of urgency about the situation. He told interviewers on CNBC, "The Fed, with its TSLF and PDCF facilities, gave the investment banks a false sense of security that they can take their time in de-levering. It slowed down the de-leveraging process, which . . . brought down Lehman, and brought Goldman and Morgan to the position they're in now. Without that bailout, I think we would be much further along in this deleveraging process and we would not be discussing a $700 billion bailout today." By devising more and greater bailout packages for Wall Street, the Fed itself slowed down and clogged the markets: "By promising ever more generous assistance—through lower interest rates, unprecedented 'liquidity' programs, and now an outright bailout—the government set up a game of chicken," writes economist Robert Murphy. "The institutions holding huge amounts of toxic assets had an incentive to drag their feet as long as possible, stringing their creditors and shareholders along, while hoping for a government miracle."[30]

By the end of the year, everyone from insurance companies to automakers was lining up for a share of the loot. The profit-and-loss system was rapidly shedding the "loss" part. More accurately, perhaps, the profit-and-loss system was beginning to mean guaranteed profits for business, and losses for taxpayers and wage-earners.

One of the most insidious consequences of the string of bailouts of the financial industry is that the American government can never credibly say that no such bailouts will ever be contemplated again. Why not? If they did it this time, why not again and again in the future? The financial industry will continue on its way in the knowledge that the big players are, in the opinion of government, "too big to fail," and so will be far more cavalier about risk than they would otherwise be. The bailout of the Big Three automakers sends the message that although mismanagement at an average-size firm will be punished with losses, gross mismanagement on a gigantic scale will be rewarded with credit and funds purloined from innocent third parties.[31] People who are good stewards of wealth are thereby forced to subsidize people who are disastrously poor stewards of wealth. It should be obvious that all the "regulation" in the world cannot prevent risky investments in an environment like this, in which moral hazard has been practically institutionalized.

And it isn't just the financial industry and American big business that are affected by moral hazard; ordinary Americans feel its effect as well. If people see that instead of foreclosure, homeowners who don't pay their mortgage receive a federal bailout, they are more likely to be careless and reckless in their own financial planning and in the timely payment of their own mortgages. If homeowners have reason to believe that the government will provide them with easier terms than their bank does, they may be tempted to stop making their mortgage payments altogether, thereby increasing the number of bad loans the federal government will have to take over. The process feeds on itself.

Ultimately, the Treasury and the Fed have been trying to prop up asset prices—i.e., keep things expensive—the best they can, hoping thereby to improve the financial health of the holders of those assets. Of course, this makes things worse for the people or companies who don't hold these assets—such as aspiring homebuyers.

Government loans to failing financial firms—and similar private loans made under government pressure—are intended to prop up these prices. But the authorities are trying to put out a fire by turning off the smoke alarm. The fall of stock prices is not the *cause* of problems in the economy. Stock prices are merely a *reflection* of the economy's condition. Artificially inflating them treats the symptom rather than the cause—the usual government response to economic crises. Financial bubbles need to burst, so that the inflated prices of the assets involved, like housing, can fall to their market prices—that is, the price on which the natural, unimpeded forces of supply and demand would converge.

The U.S. government wants to do something like the opposite: propping bubble prices up and keeping them at levels above what the market would assign, and guaranteeing the difference itself.

Perhaps the hope is that Americans will drive themselves still further into debt in order to buy, and thus validate the high prices of, luxury condos in an overextended housing market. That seems doubtful. "Shoring up prices to prevent a further debasement of overly generous loans is not designed to bring back buyers of homes and mortgage paper," says Nobel Laureate Vernon L. Smith.[32] The federal government's war on reality cannot succeed. Prices that seek to come down are going to come down.

Everything the Fed and the Treasury have tried to do amounts to treating symptoms rather than causes. Henry Paulson says falling home prices are the problem. President George W. Bush, in his address to the nation calling for the bailout, warned Americans that the value of their homes would tumble without this package, which would presumably try to prop up their prices through one mechanism or another. But falling house prices are not themselves the problem. The problem was the initial inflation of home prices by the unleashing of the Fed's credit spigot for years on end; falling home prices merely brought to light this initial distortion. They are the market's way of correcting it and revaluing asset prices rationally. So here we have the federal government, which claims to want to make housing more affordable—that, in fact, was the very reason for the creation of Fannie and Freddie in the first place—endorsing a policy of maintaining bubble prices in the real estate market. Whatever happened to the goal of affordable housing? Can a stream of rational thought be found amid all this convoluted nonsense?

When the bill comes due

The government does not have a magical supply of funds it can tap into. It will either borrow or print the money it needs for its bailouts, or seize it from the population. Some of the money may come from higher taxes, either soon or—in the case of borrowed money—in a few years. The wealth-producing sector will be that much the poorer, and all the production and investment that those funds might have brought about will be lost forever in exchange for propping up firms that deserved to go bankrupt. Alternatively, the Fed can just print more money for the Obama administration to spend, a process that makes existing money go down in value. That process had already begun by late 2008: between September and December alone, the Fed's balance sheet shot up from $900 billion to over $2.2 trillion. The *New York Times* said in mid-December that the Fed's balance sheet would soon be up to $3 trillion.[33] This uptick in the Fed's balance sheet tells us something about how much new money the Fed has created, since in order for the Fed to buy an asset that winds up on its balance sheet, it must create, out of thin air, the money to buy it. Right now, the banks are holding on to much of that new money, but as soon as they start lending it, the result will be an explosion in consumer prices, especially since every one dollar the Fed creates out of thin air is the base for the banks' own creation of $10 out of thin air. To avoid that outcome, the Fed will suddenly have to contract the money supply, thereby prolonging the chaos. (Hard to believe, I know, that a system like this, described further in chapter 6, could give rise to instability!)

Whatever the government chooses to do, the result will be to divert resources away from wealth producers, dry up healthy economic activity, and reduce the pool of resources for the private economy to use toward recovery. Those effects will be relatively invisible, since no one will know exactly which marginal firms were driven under by this last nail in their coffins. The alleged benefits, small and even undesirable as they may be, carry the benefit of being visible, and something politicans can point to. They will be the widely hailed accomplishments of President Obama.

The costs, as usual, will be dispersed and unknown, and therefore of no interest to our wise planners.

The amount the U.S. government will need to borrow, if it wants to prop up the entire financial system instead of allowing healthy bankruptcies and losses, will eventually become so great that ever fewer people and governments will want to lend it, knowing it will never be paid back. And with the entitlement collapse on its way thanks to the coming insolvency of Social Security and Medicare—another predictable crisis that everyone will pretend couldn't have been foreseen—and tens of trillions of dollars coming due on that front, something has to give. These problems cannot be papered over forever.

Meanwhile, the two major party candidates for president in 2008 were simply hopeless. Both agreed on the bailout package, naturally. John McCain, the "fiscal conservative," even proposed that the federal government buy up troubled mortgages to the potential tune of trillions of dollars. A few days later he was criticizing his opponent for funding a $3 million planetarium in Chicago, a project that cost about one-millionth as much.[34]

There's nothing particularly new or surprising about the thought process that has motivated the bailouts. Economist Lionel Robbins observed in the middle of the Great Depression, "Everywhere, in the money market, in the commodity markets and in the broad field of company finance and public indebtedness, the efforts of central banks and governments have been directed to propping up bad business positions."[35] Earlier still, Yale's William Graham Sumner observed: "For three hundred years our history has been marked by the alternations of 'prosperity' and 'distress' which are produced by the booms and their collapses. When the collapse comes, the people who are left long on goods and land [and stocks] always make a great outcry and start a political agitation. Their favorite device is to try to inflate the currency and raise prices again until they can unload.... No scheme which has ever been devised by them has ever made a collapsed boom go up again."[36]

That never stops them from trying, and today the Fed thinks pumping in more money and driving interest rates lower still—in other words,
more of the same—can solve the problem. But Ludwig von Mises
warned:

> The wavelike movement affecting the economic system, the re-
> currence of periods of boom which are followed by periods of de-
> pression, is the unavoidable outcome of the attempts, repeated
> again and again, to lower the gross market rate of interest by
> means of credit expansion. There is no means of avoiding the final
> collapse of a boom brought about by credit expansion. The alter-
> native is only whether the crisis should come sooner as the result
> of a voluntary abandonment of further credit expansion, or later
> as a final and total catastrophe of the currency system involved.

In other words, there is no shortcut to creating wealth. We cannot become prosperous by pushing interest rates lower than the market would
have set them. There is no monetary magic wand that can make everyone rich. The interest rate was at the level the market established for a
reason, and when governments and their central banks artificially interfere with it, they mislead investors into destructive courses of action they
would not otherwise have taken. They encourage investment in lines that
make no long-run sense. They encourage consumption at a time when investors are starved for capital.

Meanwhile, the free market takes the blame when these artificially
encouraged lines of investment and production go belly up. But the free
market has nothing to do with it. It is the interference with the free market, the refusal to allow the market to coordinate production and consumption, that causes the problem.

F. A. Hayek won the Nobel Prize in economics for showing how central banks—which are creatures of government, not the free market—
set the boom-bust cycle in motion when they try to take shortcuts to
prosperity.[37] There are no such shortcuts, and central banks' attempts to

pretend otherwise are destined to end in disaster. That is what happened in our case: artificially low interest rates, thanks to the Federal Reserve, encouraged lines of production that made no sense and could not be sustained in the long run.

Hayek is one Nobel Prize winner Americans need to hear, and what he had to say is the subject of the next chapter.

CHAPTER 4

HOW GOVERNMENT CAUSES
THE BOOM-BUST BUSINESS CYCLE

We take it for granted as a fact of economic life: plush times inevitably give way to lean times, and back and forth in an endless cycle. Just as the moon waxes and wanes and the tides ebb and flow, the economy goes through booms and busts.

The median home price across all U.S. cities increased by 150 percent from August of 1998 until August of 2006. Over the next two years, home prices fell by 23 precent.[1] Foreclosures and defaults skyrocketed.

The stock market has followed a similar course. When the New York Stock Exchange closed on October 9, 2007, the Dow Jones Industrial Average was 14,164.53, the highest close ever. Thirteen months later, on November 20, 2008, it closed at 7,552.29, a drop of 46.7 percent.

Busts always bring with them some personal pain. This time, the pain is more visible than usual. Retirement portfolios have been eviscerated. Unemployment has increased. By November 2008, unemployment was up to 6.7 percent. When the figures are compiled the way government calculated them in the 1970s (before it started massaging the data to make the employment picture look prettier) the unemployment rate in November was an astonishing 16.7 percent.[2]

The personal dimensions of these busts are always used to justify government intervention, whether creating a "safety net" or drawing up new regulations aimed at smoothing out the cycle that is supposedly inherent in the free market.

But is this really so inevitable? Is the market economy really prone to such sudden and inexplicable episodes of massive business error, or could something outside the market be causing it? This is not just an academic question. The American people, currently suffering as a falling tide lowers all boats, need and deserve the answer.

As politicians and our media drones talk about what to do next, they promise us ways to prevent another meltdown like the one we're suffering through now. If they're going to come close to succeeding, they need to understand the causes of the business cycle. What causes these violent swings?

If politicians are thorough and honest in seeking out a culprit, they aren't going to be pleased with what they find at the end of the trail of crumbs. It's not "capitalism." It's not "greed." It's not "deregulation." It's an institution created by government itself.

"Cluster of errors"

No one is surprised when a business has to close its doors. Businesses come and go all the time. Entrepreneurs are not infallible, and they sometimes make poor forecasts of consumer demand. They may have miscalculated their costs of production, failed to anticipate the pattern of consumer tastes, underestimated the resources necessary to comply with ever-changing government regulation, or made any number of other errors. Business failure is the inevitable consequence of our inability to know the future with certainty.

But when a great many businesses, all at once, suffer losses or have to close, that *should* surprise us. Losses suffered in a single business are one thing. Again, no one has perfect foresight. But why should so many businessmen make errors all at once? The market gradually weeds out business owners who do a poor job as stewards of capital and forecasters of consumer demand by punishing them with losses and, if their inefficiency persists, driving them out of business altogether. So why should businessmen, even those well established and who have passed the market test year after year, suddenly all make the same kind of error?

British economist Lionel Robbins argued that this "cluster of errors," as he called it, demanded explanation: "Why should the leaders of business in the various industries producing producers' goods make errors of judgment at the same time and in the same direction?"[3] We call this pattern of (apparent) business prosperity followed by general business depression the *business cycle*, the *trade cycle*, or the *boom-bust cycle*. Does it have a cause or is it, as Karl Marx tried to argue, an inherent feature of the market economy?

This question matters today because the Obama administration has ridden into town blaming "deregulation" and the market itself for the meltdown, and promising the usual government solutions. To prevent another painful bust, we need to know what set us up for this one. We need to uncover what drives the business cycle.

One clue lies in the historical fact that busts are especially severe in capital-goods industries—e.g., raw materials, construction, capital equipment, and the like—and relatively mild in the consumer goods sector: pencils, hats, picture frames. Put another way, things consumers actually buy don't suffer from busts as much as do things produced in the higher-order stages of production, farther removed from finished consumer goods. Why should this be?

How things work in a free market

The economist F. A. Hayek won the Nobel Prize in economics in 1974 for a theory of the business cycle that holds great explanatory power—especially in light of the 2008 financial crisis, which so many economists have been at a loss to explain. Hayek's work, which builds on a theory developed by economist Ludwig von Mises, finds the root of the boom-bust cycle in the central bank. In our case that's the Federal Reserve System, the very institution that postures as the protector of the economy and the source of relief from business cycles. Chapter 6 will have more to say about what the Federal Reserve is and how it operates. For now it is enough to say that the Fed, which opened its doors in 1914 after passage of the Federal Reserve Act in 1913, can expand and contract the supply of money in the economy, and can influence the movement of interest rates upward or downward.

Looking at the money supply makes sense when looking for the root of an economy-wide problem. After all, money is the one thing present in all corners of the market, as Lionel Robbins pointed out in his 1934 book *The Great Depression.* "Is it not probable," he asked, "that disturbances affecting many lines of industry at once will be found to have monetary causes?"[4]

In particular, the culprit turns out to be the central bank's interference with interest rates. Interest rates are like a price. Borrowed money, or loaned capital, is a good, and you pay a price to borrow it. When you put money in a savings account or buy a bond, you are the lender, and so the interest rate you earn is the price you are being paid for your money.

As with all goods, the *supply* of loanable funds sometimes goes up and down, and on the other hand *demand* for loanable funds goes up and down. The supply and demand determine the price. If more families are saving more or more banks are lending, borrowers don't have to pay as much to borrow—interest rates go down. If there's a rush to borrow or a dearth of loanable funds, interest rates go up.

That's what happens in a free market, where supply and demand set the price. There are some results of this dynamic, not obvious at first, that contribute to a healthy economy.

Let's start with the case in which people are saving more, thus increasing the supply of lending capital and lowering interest rates. From a business's perspective, low interest rates provide an opportunity to engage in long-term projects that would not pay off under higher interest rates. Businesses respond to the lower rates by taking the opportunity to engage in long-term projects aimed at increasing their productive capacity in the future—e.g., expanding existing facilities, building a new physical plant or acquiring new capital equipment.

Look at it also from the saver's perspective. Saving more indicates a relatively lower desire to consume in the present. This is another incentive for businesses to invest in the future, to carry out time-consuming investment projects with an eye to *future* production, rather than produce and sell things *now*.

On the other hand, if people possess an intense desire to consume right now, they will save less—making it less affordable for businesses to carry out long-term projects (because interest rates will be higher). The big supply of *consumer* dollars on the table make it a good time to produce and sell *now*.

The way to express this happy arrangement is to say that *the interest rate coordinates production across time*. It ensures a compatible mix of market forces: if people want to consume now, businesses respond accordingly; if people want to consume in the future, businesses allocate resources to satisfy that desire as well. Firms won't devote as many resources to product development, for instance, when the consuming public prefers more existing goods right now.

...But then the Fed steps in

The interest rate can perform this coordinating function only if it is allowed to move up and down freely in response to changes in supply and demand. If the Fed manipulates the interest rate, we should not be surprised to observe discoordination on a massive scale.

As we shall see later, the Fed has various tools it can use to manipulate interest rates, moving them upward or downward. Suppose it lowers them. As we've seen, on the free market, interest rates go down because the public is saving more. But when the Fed lowers rates artificially, they no longer reflect the true state of consumer demand and economic conditions in general. People have not actually increased their savings or indicated a desire to lower their present consumption. These artificially low interest rates mislead investors. They make investment decisions suddenly appear profitable that under normal conditions would be correctly assessed as unprofitable. From the point of view of the economy as a whole, irrational investment decisions are made and investment activity is distorted. The Federal Reserve's policy of cheap credit misleads businesses into thinking that now is a good time to invest in *long-term* projects. But the public has given no indication of any intention to postpone *present* consumption and free up resources that business firms can devote to those long-term projects.[5] Even if some of these projects can be finished, with the public's saving relatively low there is reason to believe the necessary purchasing power won't be around later, when businesses hope to cash in on their long-term investments.

The central bank's lowering of the interest rate therefore creates a mismatch of market forces. The coordination of production across time is disrupted. *Long-term* investments that will bear fruit *only in the distant future* are encouraged at a time when the public has shown no letup in its desire to consume *in the present*. Consumers have not chosen to save and release resources for use in the higher stages of production.* To the contrary, the lower interest rates encourage them to save less and thus *consume more*, at a time when investors are also looking to *invest more* resources. The economy is being stretched in two directions at once, and resources are therefore being misallocated into lines that cannot be sustained over the long term.

As the company works towards completing its projects, it will find that the resources it needs, such as labor, materials, replacement parts—called by economists "complementary factors of production"—are not

---

*What does it mean to say consumers "release" resources for use in the higher-order stages of production? Think of your income as your compensation for goods and services you have produced or helped produce. The less of that money you use to enter the economy and claim goods for your own use and the more of it you save, the larger is the pool of real savings from which producers can draw.

available in sufficient quantities. The pool of real savings turns out to be smaller than entrepreneurs anticipated, and thus the complementary factors of production they need wind up being scarcer than they expected. The prices for these parts, labor, and other resources will therefore be higher than entrepreneurs expected, and business costs will rise. Firms will need to borrow more to finance these unanticipated increases in input prices. This increased demand for borrowing will raise the interest rate. Reality now begins to set in: some of these projects cannot be completed. The economy is not yet wealthy enough to fund them all, although the artificially low interest rate had misled investors into thinking it was.

The economy, in other words, can support only so many investment projects at once. The interest rate acts as the market's restraint on how many such projects are begun, in order to prevent the initiation of more projects than the pool of savings can support in the long run. When the interest rate is *artificially* lowered, more loans can be extended and more projects *started*, but artificially low interest rates do not magically supply the additional real resources necessary to complete all the projects.[6]

Moreover, the *kind* of projects that are started differ from those that would have been started on the free market. Mises draws an analogy between an economy under the influence of artificially low interest rates and a home builder who falsely believes he has more resources—more bricks, say—than he really does. He will build a house whose size and proportions are different from the ones he would have chosen if he had known his true supply of bricks. He will not be able to complete this larger house with the number of bricks he has. The sooner he discovers his true brick supply the better, for then he can adjust his production plans before too much of the finished house is produced and too many of his labor and material resources are squandered. If he finds out only toward the very final stages of the project, he will have to destroy almost the entire house, and both he and society at large will be so much the poorer for his malinvestment of all those resources.[7]

In the short run the result of the central bank's lowering of interest rates is the apparent prosperity of the boom period. Stocks and real estate shoot up. New construction is everywhere, businesses are expanding their capacity, and people are enjoying a high standard of living. But the economy is on a sugar high, and reality inevitably sets in. Some of these investments will prove to be unsustainable and will have to be abandoned, with the resources devoted to them having been partially or completely squandered.[8]

Keynes's fantasy: Permanent boom

That is one of the reasons the Fed cannot simply pump more credit into the economy and keep the boom going.[9] Yet the economist John Maynard Keynes—who is oddly back in fashion in Washington (even though his system collapsed in the early 1970s when it couldn't account for "stagflation")—proposed exactly this: "The remedy for the boom is not a higher rate of interest but a lower rate of interest! For that may enable the so-called boom to last. The right remedy for the trade cycle is not to be found in abolishing booms and thus keeping us permanently in a semi-slump; but in abolishing slumps and keeping us permanently in a quasi-boom."[10]

As usual, Keynes was dealing in fantasy. The more the Fed inflates, the worse the eventual reckoning will be.[11] Every new wave of additional artificial credit deforms the capital structure still further, making the inevitable bust all the more severe, because so much more capital will have been squandered and so many more resources misallocated.

The more the process is allowed to go on, the further along the economy moves in its unsustainable direction, just as the house builder from Mises' example gets himself into deeper trouble the more he works on the house while under a false impression of how many bricks he has left. He could have built a house successfully with the bricks he had on hand, but thinking he has more than he really does, he goes about building a different kind of house, and one which he lacks the necessary resources to complete.

As it becomes clear that so much of the boom is unsustainable in the long run, pressure builds for liquidation of the malinvestments—that is, they need to be discontinued, the equipment sold off. The misdirected capital, if salvageable, needs to be freed up for other enterprises where it is more urgently needed. Should the Fed ignore this pressure and simply carry on inflating the money supply, Mises warned, it runs the risk of hyperinflation, a severe, galloping inflation that destroys the currency unit altogether.*

Writing during the Great Depression, F. A. Hayek scolded those who thought they could inflate their way out of the disaster, keeping interest rates pushed down indefinitely:

> Instead of furthering the inevitable liquidation of the maladjustments brought about by the boom during the last three years, all conceivable means have been used to prevent that readjustment from taking place; and one of these means, which has been repeatedly tried though without success, from the earliest to the most recent stages of depression, has been this deliberate policy of credit expansion....
>
> To combat the depression by a forced credit expansion is to attempt to cure the evil by the very means which brought it about; because we are suffering from a misdirection of production, we want to create further misdirection—a procedure that

---

*Hyperinflation or the central bank's cessation of its cheap credit policy out of a fear of hyperinflation are not the only two ways the bust can come. The artificially low interest rates stimulate venture capital (long-term investment) and consumer-good production (short-term investment), stretching the economy at both ends at the expense of the middle (capital maintenance, or medium-term investment). If the government tries to keep the boom going by continually pumping in new money, the undermaintenance of existing capital will eventually impinge on the economy's ability to keep consumers supplied with current consumables. Alternatively stated, market forces will eventually reallocate resources away from venture capital and current consumables toward capital maintenance, thus ending the boom. For an easy-to-understand example of this process, see Robert P. Murphy, "The Importance of Capital Theory," October 20, 2008, http://mises.org/story/3155.

can only lead to a much more severe crisis as soon as the credit expansion comes to an end. . . . It is probably to this experiment, together with the attempts to prevent liquidation once the crisis had come, that we owe the exceptional severity and duration of the depression.[12]

The recession or depression is the necessary if unfortunate correction process by which the malinvestments of the boom period, having at last been brought to light, are finally liquidated, redeployed elsewhere in the economy where they can contribute to producing something consumers actually want. No longer are wealth and goods diverted into unsustainable investments with inadequate demand and insufficient resources. Businesses fail and investment projects are abandoned.

Although painful for many people, the recession or depression phase of the cycle is not where the damage is done. The bust is the period in which the economy sloughs off the malinvestments and the capital misallocation, re-establishes the structure of production along sustainable lines, and restores itself to health. The damage is done during the *boom* phase, the period of false prosperity that precedes the bust. It is then that the artificial lowering of interest rates causes the misdirection of capital and the initiation of unsustainable investments. It is then that resources that would genuinely have satisfied consumer demand are diverted into projects that make sense only in light of the temporary and artificial conditions of the boom. For the mistaken bricklayer, the damage wasn't done when he tore down the walls of the excessively large house he could never complete; the damage was done when he laid the bricks too broadly. Nobody likes unemployment and bankruptcy, of course, but they would not have been necessary had the artificial boom not been stimulated in the first place.

As we can now see, the Austrian theory successfully answers our two original questions. The "cluster of errors" occurs because an artificially low interest rate systematically misleads economic actors, who make investment decisions as if more saved resources exist in the economy than actually do. Since these resources do not in fact exist, not all of the newly undertaken investment projects can be completed. The downturn is heavier in producer-goods industries than in consumer-goods industries because that sector is the most sensitive to interest-rate changes, and therefore disproportionately attracts investment.[13]

Investment adviser Peter Schiff draws an analogy between an artificial boom and a circus that comes to town for a few weeks. When the circus arrives, its performers and the crowds it attracts patronize local restaurants and businesses. Now suppose a restaurant owner mistakenly concludes that this boom in his business will endure permanently. He may respond by building an addition, or perhaps even opening a second location. But as soon as the circus leaves town, our businessman finds he has tragically miscalculated.[14]

Does it make sense to try to inflate this poor businessman's way out of his predicament? In other words, should the banking system create new money out of thin air to lend to him to keep his business profitable? Creating new money doesn't create any new stuff, so lending this business owner newly created money merely allows him to draw more of the economy's existing resource pool to himself, at the expense of genuine businesses that actually cater to real consumer wishes. Getting him hooked on cheap credit only prolongs the misallocation of resources. This restaurant is a bubble activity that can survive only under the phony conditions of what we might call the circus-induced boom. It needs to come to an end, so that the resources it employs can be reallocated to more sensible lines of production.

One more point is important to remember: *all* firms are affected by the artificial boom, not just those that embarked on new investment projects or that came into existence in the first place only thanks to artificially cheap credit. By the peak of the dot-com boom in the year 2000, for example, Microsoft—which had been established long before the boom—found itself face to face with the shortage of factors of production that Austrian theory predicts; the company began having a difficult time finding and keeping employees, especially in Silicon Valley.[15] Mises observed that "in order to continue production on the enlarged scale brought about by the expansion of credit, *all entrepreneurs*, those who did expand their activities no less than those who produce only within the limits in which they produced previously, need additional funds as the costs of production are now higher."[16]

Notice that the precipitating factor in the business cycle has nothing to do with the market economy itself. It is the government's policy of pushing interest rates below the level at which the free market would have set them. The central bank is a government institution, established by government legislation, whose personnel are appointed by government and which enjoys government-granted monopoly privileges. It bears repeating: the central bank's interventions into the economy give rise to the business cycle, and *the central bank is not a free-market institution.*

The theory restated

Here, in a very simple summary, is what the Austrian theory says:

1) Interest rates can come down in two ways: a) the public saves more; or b) the central bank artificially forces them down.

2) Businessmen respond to the lower interest rates by starting new projects. The projects tend to be those that are the most interest-rate sensitive—in particular, they occur in the so-called higher-order stages of production: mining, raw materials, construction, capital equipment, etc. Production processes farthest removed in time from finished consumer goods, in other words.

3a) If the interest rate is lower because of natural causes—e.g., increased saving—then the market works smoothly. People's deferred consumption provides the material wherewithal for businesses' new investment projects to be seen through to completion.

3b) If the interest rate is lower because of artificial causes—e.g., the manipulation by a central bank—then these projects cannot all be completed. The necessary resources to complete them have not been saved by the public. Investors have been misled into production lines that cannot be sustained.

4) Imagine a home builder who believes he has 20 percent more bricks than he actually has. He will build a different kind of house than he would if he had an accurate count of his brick supply. (Assume he can't buy any more.) The dimensions will be different. The style may even be different. And the longer he goes without realizing his error, the worse the eventual reckoning will be. If he finds out his error only at the very end, he'll have to tear down the whole (incomplete) house, and all those resources and labor time will have been squandered. Society will be that much the poorer.

5) The economy is like the home builder. Forcing interest rates lower than the free market would have set them makes economic actors act as if more saved resources exist than actually do. Some portion of their new investment is malinvestment—investment in lines that would have made sense if the saved resources existed to sustain and complete them, but which do not make sense in light of current resource availability.

6) The housing boom is a classic example of this theory in action. Artificially low interest rates misdirected enormous resources into home construction. We now know that was unsustainable. There were only so many $900,000 homes that the public, which had been saving very little, was in a position to buy.

7) The sooner the monetary manipulation comes to an end, the sooner the malinvestment can be shaken out and misallocated resources redirected into sustainable lines. The longer we try to prop things up, the worse the inevitable bust will be. The home builder in our example would have been much better off if he had discovered his error sooner, because far fewer resources would have been irrevocably squandered. The same goes for the economy at large.

The longer you hold on, the more it hurts

A reasonable objection to the Austrian explanation runs as follows: why can't businessmen simply learn to distinguish between low interest rates that reflect an increase in genuine savings, and low interest rates that reflect nothing more than Fed manipulation? Why do they not learn

Austrian business cycle theory and then avoid expanding when the Fed tries to ignite an artificial boom?

The answer is that it is not so easy. (First of all, even most *economists* are unaware of Austrian business cycle theory, and it is a rare business school in which the subject is taught.) Even businessmen who do know the Austrian theory and who know with absolute certainty that the Fed is keeping interest rates artificially low may still find it in their interest to borrow and launch new projects, hoping their project will be one of the lucky ones and that they can get out well before the bust hits. If they sit back and do nothing, and do not react to the lower rates, their competitors surely will, and might be able to gain market share at their expense. Someone will take the bait.

The Austrian theory of the business cycle does not, and is not intended to, account for the length and persistence of a depression. It is a theory of the artificial boom, which culminates in the bust. The bust period is longer the more government prevents the economy from reallocating labor and capital into a sustainable pattern of production. Government interference, in the form of wage or price controls, emergency lending, additional "liquidity," further monetary inflation, and so on—all aimed at diminishing short-term pain—exacerbate the long-term agony.

Attempts to inflate the economy out of the downturn by pumping in more money created out of thin air and thereby keeping interest rates artificially low only make the eventual and inevitable collapse—which, modern superstitions notwithstanding, cannot be held off indefinitely by monetary trickery—all the more severe. The malinvestments need to be discontinued and liquidated, not encouraged and subsidized, if the economy's capital structure is to return to a sustainable condition.

There will always be those who, not understanding the situation, will call for still more and greater monetary injections in order to try to keep the boom going, but their number has skyrocketed since the fall of 2008. Pointon York strategist Roger Nightingale was far from alone in 2008 in urging the world's central banks to lower interest rates to *zero*. "I'm not talking about 50 basis points," he said. "We really have to take rates down to effectively zero. . . . The Europeans have to go to zero, the Brits have to go very close to zero, the Japanese of course haven't got much room, they certainly have to go to zero." He added that even zero might not be low enough. Bank of England governor Mervyn King said he was ready to reduce rates to "whatever level is necessary," including as low as zero.[17]

In other downturns, everyone would have understood this to be, well, crazy. Today, so many of our financial analysts have taken leave of their senses that we hear zero interest rates, the Keynesian dream, discussed as if it were a serious policy proposal. Such an uncomprehending suggestion would merely perpetuate and aggravate the resource misallocations of the boom and set the stage for a far worse crisis in the future. (But since uncomprehending suggestions seem to be driving American economic policy right now, we should not be surprised that the Fed itself made the move to zero interest rates in mid-December 2008, setting its federal-funds rate target at 0 to 0.25 percent.)[18]

Likewise, there must be no attempt to prop up prices or wages. Resources and laborers need to be directed into those lines of production in which the healthy, non-bubble economy needs them. When prices and wages are made artificially rigid, this process is disrupted and the return to prosperity delayed. Contrary to popular belief, wages were rather high during the Great Depression. But that was the problem—they were *artificially* high, thanks to government intervention, and therefore far fewer people were hired in the first place.

The folly of public-works stimulus

Keynesian "pump-priming," whereby governments fund "public works" projects, often financed by deficits, is another destructive if inexplicably fashionable course of action, based on the modern superstition that the very act of spending, on anything at all, is the path to economic health. This is the root of the "stimulus" packages that Democrats typically want to implement. (The Republican version involves printing up money out of thin air and then sending out checks, an equally counterproductive strategy.) *Take from the economy as a whole and pour resources into particular sectors—that should make us rich!* Economic historian Robert Higgs compared plans like these to someone taking water from the deep end of a pool, pouring it into the shallow end, and expecting the water level to rise.

The economy is trying to readjust the allocation of capital and labor across the various stages of production, liquidating those concerns that are squandering wealth and directing resources into those lines in which healthy expansion is possible. Additional public-works spending is one of the last things the economy needs, for it (1) deprives the private sector of resources by taxing people to support these projects; (2) diverts resources toward firms that themselves may need to be liquidated; and (3) artificially drives *up* interest rates (if the projects are funded by government borrowing), thereby making bank credit more difficult to come by for firms that are actually producing things consumers have freely indicated they want.

In addition to all that, these projects are the very opposite of what the fragile economy of the bust calls for. It needs to shift resources swiftly into the production of goods in line with consumer demand and with as little resource waste as possible. Government, on the other hand, has no non-arbitrary way of knowing how much of something to produce, where to produce it, using what materials and which production methods. Private firms use a profit-and-loss test to gauge how well they are meeting consumer needs. If they make profits, the market has ratified their production decisions. They have efficiently combined their inputs to create a finished product that consumers value more than they valued the sum of the inputs. If they post losses, that means they have squandered resources that could have been more effectively employed on behalf of consumer welfare elsewhere in the economy. Government has no such feedback mechanism, since it acquires its resources not through voluntary means, as in the private sector, but through seizure from the citizens, and no one can choose to buy or not to buy what the government produces with those resources. The purpose of production on the market is to satisfy real consumer demands; politically motivated and economically arbitrary diversions of resources do absolutely nothing to set the economy on a long-run path of accomplishing that. So these projects squander wealth at a time of falling living standards and a need for the greatest possible efficiency with existing resources.

The state must also resist the temptation to extend any form of emergency credit to failing businesses. If their positions are sound, credit will be forthcoming from the private sector. If not, then they should go out of business, freeing up resources to be used by more capable stewards. Diverting resources from those who have successfully met consumer demands to those who have not serves only to weaken the economy still further and make recovery that much more difficult. Society is made worse off, not better off, by subsidizing loans and channeling resources to the restaurant owner who thought the circus would never leave.

The dot-com boom

Prior to the present crisis, the so-called dot-com boom was the last example of the Austrian theory in action in American history.

August 9, 1995, was an extraordinary day for Netscape, the company that created the then-popular web browser of the same name. It was the company's initial public offering (IPO), the first day it was to offer shares for sale to the public. By the end of the day it was trading at $75 a share, nearly three times the $28 where it began. The company had not yet posted a dollar of profit, but co-founder Jim Clark's 20 percent stake in the company was suddenly worth $663 million.

Netscape's IPO has often been identified as the start of the Internet or dot-com boom, a five-year period in which Internet startup companies saw their stock prices soar, only to come crashing down to reality in the year 2000. In these heady days, Alan Greenspan began arguing that a "New Economy" had arrived, in which previous constraints no longer held, and booms did not have to end in busts. But to the contrary, the dot-com boom did end in a bust, along the precise lines predicted by Austrian business cycle theory.

All the elements are there. There were low interest rates brought about by the Fed's expansionary monetary policy: the money supply grew by 52 percent between June 1995 and March 2000 (as measured by a metric called "Money Zero Maturity" or MZM), at a time when real GDP growth was only 22 percent.[19] Over time these companies found that the complementary capital goods they needed—such as web programmers, Silicon Valley real estate, and Internet domain names— were unexpectedly scarce, and thus rising in price. The government's price indexes showed low to moderate price inflation during the years of the dot-com boom, but had no way to reflect the dramatic rise in the *specific prices* of concern to dot-com firms—a case of statistical aggregates concealing what is truly relevant and interesting. It was the rise in these specific prices that made the dot-com boom so difficult to sustain.

Austrian business cycle theory describes an economy in which (1) malinvestment has occurred, and more projects have been begun than can be completed in light of current resources, and in which at the same time (2) an excess of consumption has taken place. That is precisely what the data from the dot-com boom reveals: the American savings rate was negative by the year 2000 and households' outstanding debt as a percentage of income was hitting all-time highs, while at the same time investment in the Bay Area was 233 percent higher than trend.[20] With consumers not saving, and in fact falling into ever greater debt, the necessary resources to complete these investment projects were not being released. This mismatch could not persist.

The condition of the NASDAQ (where most of the dot-com stocks traded) during these years strongly suggested that this sector had been distorted and inflated by the Fed's easy credit policy. The price-to-earnings (P/E) ratios of the over-the-counter securities of the NASDAQ are normally relatively low, usually around ten or less, meaning you could theoretically buy up 100 percent of the company's stock by paying about ten times the company's annual earnings. By the late

1990s many of these prices were hundreds of times their earnings (if indeed they had any earnings at all!).[21] It was at this time that Alan Greenspan was arguing that it was impossible at a given moment to know if a financial bubble existed. These dot-com stocks sent the NASDAQ tumbling in the year 2000, when it suffered a 40 percent decline.[22]

Between June 1999 and May 2000 the Fed began to tighten credit, raising the discount rate six times. Some commentators complained that Greenspan had derailed the dot-com boom and torpedoed the "new economy," which could have persisted into the indefinite future had the Fed not turned down the monetary spigot. That is not true. Dramatically rising prices for the factors of production on which the boom depended—from network engineers and technical managers to office space and housing for workers—had to bring it to an end eventually. Programmers' salaries more than doubled during the boom. Coveted domain names skyrocketed: while tv.com sold for $15,000 in 1996, by 1997 business.com was selling for $150,000. Few entrepreneurs could have expected that degree of sector-specific spikes in prices.[23]

It was in response to the dot-com and NASDAQ collapses and the modest recession that accompanied them that Alan Greenspan and the Fed chose to embark on a robust policy of inflation, an approach that began in early 2001, which saw no fewer than eleven rate cuts, and culminated in lowering the federal funds rate (the rate at which banks lend to each other) to a mere 1 percent from June 2003 to June 2004.[24] That year alone saw eleven rate cuts. The unsustainable dot-com boom could not, in the end, be reignited, and thank goodness—the resource misallocations in that sector were unhealthy for the economy. But the Fed's easy money and refusal to allow the recession of 2000 to take its course led to an even more perilous bubble elsewhere. That was the only recession on record in which housing starts did not decline.[25] Not coincidentally, that was also the moment at which people began to buy into the bromides of the housing bubble: housing prices never fall, a house is the best investment one can make, house-flipping is a safe and easy way to make a living, and all the other delusions to which the Fed-created bubble gave rise.[26] By intervening in the market, the Fed only postponed what it was trying to avoid, and made the crash worse when it finally came.

The Japanese bust

Similarly, the 1980s saw a spectacular boom in Japan financed in large part by inflationary credit expansion—that is, the creation of money out of thin air through the banking system and the artificial lowering of interest rates that accompanies the increased money supply. When the inevitable bust came, it hit hard. The Nikkei, the Japanese stock market, dropped from 40,000 in late 1989 to 15,000 in 1992. Real estate prices dropped 80 percent between 1991 and 1998. All the while, the Bank of Japan and the Japanese government more generally did everything they could to prevent the liquidation and try to prop up prices and bad debt. They pushed interest rates all the way to zero. They obstructed market correction of the malinvestments of the boom. The structure of production therefore remained stuck in a pattern that did not correspond to consumer demand. As a result, Japan had an economic depression of its own for well over a decade.

A valuable piece of evidence in favor of the Austrian account of what happened to Japan's economy emerges when we examine the sectors that were hardest hit by the recession. If Austrian business cycle theory is correct, we should expect the most significant declines to be in the capital-intensive industries in the higher-order stages of production.[27] And that is exactly what the data shows. In order from most capital intensive and farthest from finished consumer goods to least capital intensive are mining, manufacturing, wholesale and retail, and the service industry. And that is also the order, from most to least, in which these industries suffered during the downturn.[28] Industries in the earliest stages of production suffered from the worst growth rates throughout the 1990s.

None of the traditional interventionist tools that supposedly bring about economic recovery—every one of which is being peddled before Americans today—did a single thing to revive her fortunes. What did Japan try? Increases in the money supply, interest-rate cuts, trillions of yen in public works spending (being proposed as part of a new "stimu-

lus package" for the United States as this book is being written), other
increases in government spending, government lending to business, and
bailouts (and even outright nationalization) of some banks. That should
sound pretty familiar, since these are the very proposals that supporters
of the free market are being ridiculed for not accepting. The Japanese
government set up a 20-trillion yen guarantee fund for zombie companies that were on their way to going bust. According to the Economic
Intelligence Unit, funds "disbursed under the program are often going
to companies that are not creditworthy and that would otherwise go
bankrupt"—in other words, precisely the firms that need to be liquidated
during the recession, and with which healthy firms are forced to compete
for resources if they are artificially kept alive.[29]

Mechanisms were put in place by which the Japanese government itself would buy up shares in order to boost stock prices should the Nikkei
drop below a certain level. During the 1990s the Japanese government
launched no fewer than ten fiscal stimulus packages at a total cost of over
100 trillion yen. None of them worked. In addition to keeping the Japanese economy in the doldrums, these packages also put Japan in terrible
fiscal shape, with its national debt (including various kinds of "off-bud-
get" debt) in excess of 200 percent of GDP.[30] In order to get banks lending again, the Bank of Japan pumped money into the banking system at
an extraordinary rate between 2001 and 2003—in April 2002, the yearly
rate of growth was 293 percent. It didn't work. During those years bank
loans averaged a 4.5 percent annual decrease.[31]

All of these activities distort market processes and hinder the reallo-
cation of resources that needs to occur as a boom comes to an end and a
bust begins to set in.

The public works programs were especially extensive. According to
Paul Krugman, who supports such programs:

> Think of it as the WPA [Works Progress Administration] on
> steroids. Over the past decade Japan has used enormous public
> works projects as a way to create jobs and pump money into the
> economy. The statistics are awesome. In 1996 Japan's public

works spending, as a share of GDP, was more than four times
that of the United States. Japan poured as much concrete as we
did, though it has a little less than half our population and 4 percent of our land area. One Japanese worker in 10 was employed
in the construction industry, far more than in other advanced
countries.[32]

With an effort of this size and scope having failed, the best Krugman
could do was to argue, lamely, that in the absence of these programs the
situation would have been worse. The opposite is true: had government
not distorted the market so severely and seized all these resources for its
own uneconomic use, the private sector would have been in a much
healthier position to build toward recovery.

One thing these programs did succeed in doing was to plunge Japan
very deeply into debt. Japan's deficit spending, says Krugman, has
"pushed Japan's debt above 130 percent of GDP. That's the highest ratio
among advanced nations, considerably worse than either Belgium or
Italy, the traditional champions. It's almost twice the advanced-country
average and 2.5 times the figure for the United States."[33]

In short, the Japanese government did absolutely everything the Austrian theory suggests it should not do in order to fight recession. It engaged in every single activity that Keynesians like Paul Krugman
recommended. As a result, its slump went on for a decade and a half.
Keynesians continue to recommend these very policies for the United
States, as if the debacle in Japan never occurred. In late 2008 financial
newspapers in the U.S. actually began to speak of a revival of Keyne-
sianism (claiming, absurdly enough, that the present crisis gave the ideas
of Keynes, one of the twentieth century's collection of inexplicably re-
spected crackpots, a new lease on life), again with no mention of Japan.

Do manias cause bubbles?

One argument has it that economic bubbles, sectors of the economy
in which prices are artificially high, are caused by psychological factors

that lead people to become irrationally committed to the production of particular kinds of goods—dot-com startups and new houses being perhaps the readiest examples in our own time. Such explanations may play a role in determining exactly *which path* the business cycle will take and which *specific assets* will be overvalued, but they cannot by themselves explain the bubble economy. Manias may steer over-investment in one direction or another, but it's the Federal Reserve pressing the accelerator.

Ludwig von Mises reminds us that a sudden drive for a particular kind of investment will raise the prices of complementary factors of production—in the case of the dot-coms, for instance, the salaries of programmers and the costs of coveted domain names—as well as the interest rate itself. In order for a mania-driven boom to persist, there would have to be an increasing supply of credit in order to fund it, since investments in that sector would grow steadily more costly over time. That could not occur in the absence of credit expansion.[34]

Even Anna Schwartz, a monetarist and not an Austrian, argues that describing something as a "mania" is no explanation at all, and that only expansionary monetary policy by the central bank can account for these phenomena:

> If you investigate individually the manias that the market has so dubbed over the years, in every case, it was expansive monetary policy that generated the boom in an asset. The particular asset varied from one boom to another. But the basic underlying propagator was too-easy monetary policy and too-low interest rates that induced ordinary people to say, well, it's so cheap to acquire whatever is the object of desire in an asset boom, and go ahead and acquire that object. And then of course if monetary policy tightens, the boom collapses.[35]

What it all means

The Austrian theory of the business cycle, the single most important piece of economic knowledge for Americans right now, has great explanatory power. It also exonerates the free market of blame for the boom-bust cycle, since the factors that bring the cycle about—the artificially low interest rates that provoke the boom, and the foolish government interventions that prolong the bust—are all examples of *interference* with the free market. Critics of the market who ignore the arguments raised in this chapter are, to say the least, not being honest.

The Austrian theory can also be helpfully applied to the study of history, and boom-bust cycles that have occurred in the past. It can even account for the Great Depression, an episode that some economists have gone so far as to suggest had "no obvious cause at all."[36] It is to that subject that we now turn.

CHAPTER 5

GREAT MYTHS ABOUT THE GREAT DEPRESSION

The New Deal, the raft of programs Franklin D. Roosevelt signed into law to fight the Great Depression, is making a comeback. Barack Obama has promised us in effect a New New Deal, and *Time* placed him on the cover as our new FDR.

At the same time, myths about the 1920s, long since discarded by reputable historians, are making a predictable comeback at the hands of ambitious politicians who seek to malign the free market and grab additional powers for themselves—in order to save us, of course.

Hoover sank the United States into the Depression, we're told, by his callous, ideologically blinkered fidelity to the laissez-faire economics favored by big business. FDR rescued us through massive government spending, public works, and regulation that saved capitalism from itself. The Great Depression's length and depth could not have been mitigated any further, and the fact that we escaped at all was thanks to the New Deal.

None of this is even slightly true. Hoover was no free-marketeer. His unprecedented interventions took the 1929 downturn and made it into the Great Depression. And as more and more scholars are belatedly coming to recognize, FDR's New Deal only prolonged it.

Just as Austrian theory suggests, the Fed's mischief was responsible for the Great Depression. Since that argument often invites the reply that boom and bust occurred in American history well before the Fed was created, we'll start by looking briefly at previous busts to see how well they conform to the theory. We'll also find it useful to compare what happened in 1920, when government allowed the economy to readjust in the wake of an inflationary boom, to what happened in 1929, when the government decided, in the name of easing the pain, to do whatever it could to interfere with the economy's readjustment.

Might there be a lesson for us here?

Boom and bust before the Fed

The previous chapter pinned the blame for the boom-bust cycle on the Federal Reserve System, in line with the Mises-Hayek theory that won the 1974 Nobel Prize. But what about boom-bust cycles that took place in American history before the Fed was created? These previous cycles were also characterized by massive credit expansions followed by busts, and are very much in line with what Hayek and Mises teach us about business cycles.[1] The pattern is so pervasive that only with serious effort could one fail to see it.

The Panic of 1819 resulted from the excessive issue of paper money by banks at all levels. This issuing of money did not correspond to gold in their vaults. When these unsound banks came crashing down, they created severe disruption in the economy as a whole. Chartered by the U.S. government in 1816, the Second Bank of the United States, the country's second national bank, had joined in this overissue of paper money, and became an engine of inflation in its own right. Hard-money critics condemned the Bank on these grounds.[2] Senator William Wells of Delaware had predicted this outcome during the debates over the chartering of the

Bank. A national bank, he cautioned, instead of serving as a check on the state banks, would simply add another layer of paper money creation to the system.[3]

In the wake of the Panic, many American writers argued that the banking system would be stable only under a system of 100 percent reserves rather than fractional reserves, and no artificial credit creation. In other words, if banks were not allowed to print up and lend out more paper money claims to gold than corresponded to actual gold in their vaults, neither artificial bubbles nor runs on banks could occur. (William Gouge, in turn, adopted this position in *A Short History of Money and Banking* [1833], one of the great nineteenth-century treatises on money and banking.) When the crisis hit, supporters of hard money typically held that government should allow events to unfold without hindrance, so that prosperity could be promptly restored. The *New York Evening Post* advised: "Time and the laws of trade will restore things to an equilibrium, if legislatures do not rashly interfere to the natural course of events."[4]

A number of voices argued at the time that the economic downturn had had a monetary cause. The banks had inflated the money supply, thus pushing up prices. Higher prices in the U.S. encouraged Americans to buy more goods abroad instead, and in turn discouraged foreigners from buying American goods. Foreigners piling up American bank notes began to demand specie (precious metal, in this case gold) for them, and specie began flowing out of the United States. This specie outflow forced the banks, which were now losing their gold reserves, to contract their loans. The contraction punctured the boom, which became a bust. Had the banks not inflated the money supply in the first place, the artificial boom and the economic chaos it ultimately led to would not have occurred.[5]

As in later crises, banks were allowed to suspend specie payment (a fancy way of saying that the law permitted them to refuse to hand over their depositors' money when their customers came looking for it) while permitting them to carry on their operations. The knowledge that government could be counted on to bail out the banks in this way created a lingering problem of moral hazard that affected banks' behavior in the future. Why be careful and honest when you can make a fortune being reckless and irresponsible, in the expectation that the government will ride to your rescue?

During the 1830s, the Second Bank of the United States orchestrated an inflationary boom that led to an inevitable bust. The Jacksonian editorial writer William Leggett had figured out the rudiments of the business cycle by the 1830s, when his editorials pointed to artificial bank credit as the culprit in the boom-bust cycle. He warned that "the alternate inflations and contractions of the paper currency incident to such a pernicious system as ours will continue to produce their inevitable consequence, unwholesome activity of business, followed by prostration, sudden and disastrous."[6] His analysis of business downturns closely anticipated Austrian business cycle theory:

What has been, what ever must be, the consequences of such a sudden and prodigious inflation of the currency? Business stimulated to the most unhealthy activity; a vast amount of over production in the mechanic arts; a vast amount of speculation in property of every kind and name, at fictitious values; and finally, a vast and terrific crash, when the treacherous and unsustainable basis crumbles beneath the stupendous fabric of credit, and the structure falls to the ground, burying in its ruins thousands who exulted in the fancied security of their elevation. Men, nowadays, go to bed deeming themselves rich, and wake in the morning to find themselves stripped of even the little they really had. They count, deluded creatures! on the continued liberality of the banks, whose persuasive entreaties seduced them into the slippery paths of speculation [think here of house flipping and the housing bubble]. But they have now to learn that the banks cannot help them if they would, and would not if they could. They were free enough to lend their aid when assistance is not needed;

but now, when it is indispensable to carry out the projects which would not have been undertaken but for the temptations they held forth, no further resources can be supplied.[7]

Writing in December 1837, Leggett observed:

Any person who has soberly observed the course of events for the last three years must have foreseen the very state of things which now exists....He will see that the banks...have been striving, with all their might, each emulating the other, to force their issues into circulation, and flood the land with their wretched substitute for money. He will see that they have used every art of cajolery and allurement to entice men to accept their proffered aid; that, in this way, they gradually excited a thirst for speculation, which they sedulously stimulated, until it increased to a delirious fever, and men, in the epidemic frenzy of the hour, wildly rushed upon all sorts of desperate adventures. They dug canals, where no commerce asked for the means of transportation; they opened roads, where no travelers desired to penetrate; and they built cities where there were none to inhabit....[8]

Leggett would not have been surprised at efforts to blame our own crisis on speculators, greedy businessmen, and the usual bogeymen. During an economic bust, he said, the average person "is bewildered in his attempts to investigate the cause of the confusion, and is ready to listen to any explanation that fixes the blame of the disaster on those whom he had previously regarded with dislike."[9]

To prevent the return of the panics and recessions he had lived through, which he expressly and repeatedly blamed on artificial credit expansion, Leggett called for a system of free banking, in which a bank was treated like any other firm and not rescued with special legal assistance and bailouts whenever it should behave irresponsibly. Strict competition would thereby force banks to be honest in their issuance of paper money, printing only as much as corresponded to the precious metals in their vaults. With other institutions having no particular interest in piling up a given bank's paper notes, the banks will encounter constant demands for redemption in specie, and those demands will force them to remain honest. That was what the experience of the 1830s taught him.

The Panic of 1857 was the result of a five-year boom based on very substantial credit expansion. Not surprisingly, the most capital-intensive industries of that decade, railroad construction and mining companies, expanded the most during the boom.[10] States had even backed railroad bonds, promising to make good on those bonds if the railroad companies did not. President James Buchanan chose to allow the liquidation to run its course, observing in his first annual message: "It is apparent that our existing misfortunes have proceeded solely from our extravagant and vicious system of paper money and bank credits." Buchanan later cautioned that as long as banks were permitted to expand credit beyond the level of deposits they held on reserve, "these revulsions must continue to occur at regular intervals."[11]

The monetary system established by the National Banking Acts of 1863 and 1864 has been described as "a quasi-central banking type of monetary system."[12] This inflationary system once again set in motion a boom-bust cycle along the Austrian-predicted pattern, culminating in the Panic of 1873 and subsequent recession. The years leading up to the Panic of 1873 saw a railroad boom, encouraged partly by credit expansion and partly by special government favors like land grants and low-interest loans. By extension, the economy also saw related booms in iron, transport, and labor rates, along with price increases in those areas. Finance professor Michael Rozeff compares it to the boom in housing in our own day, which was also promoted by a combination of regulatory and monetary factors.[13]

And in any event, the poor condition of the American economy in the 1870s has often been exaggerated. The decade ending in 1879 saw 6.8 percent real national product growth per annum and a 4.5 percent average annual increase in real product per capita. U.S. Census statistics show manufacturing employment increasing from 2.47 million in 1870 to 3.29 million in 1880. The agricultural labor force is listed as having increased from 12.9 million to 17.4 million during the same time.[14] What appears to have made historians conceive of this period as one of unmitigated "depression" is the ongoing decrease in the price level by about 3.8 percent per annum. The trouble, according to economist Murray Rothbard, is that "most historians and economists are conditioned to believe that steadily and sharply falling prices *must* result in depression: hence their amazement at the obvious prosperity and economic growth during this era."[15] Milton Friedman and Anna Schwartz, who are not inclined to an Austrian perspective, suggested something similar about the 1870s:

> The contraction was long and it was severe—of that there is no doubt. But the sharp decline in financial magnitudes, so much more obvious and so much better documented than the behavior of a host of poorly measured physical magnitudes, may well have led contemporary observers and later students to overestimate the severity of the contraction and perhaps even its length. Observers of the business scene then, no less then their modern descendants, took it for granted that sharply declining prices were incompatible with sharply rising output. The period deserves much more study than it has received precisely because it seems to run sharply counter to such strongly held views.[16]

Yale University's William Graham Sumner, writing during the 1870s, identified the fallacy behind the inflationist schemes that had brought about so much economic carnage in American history and in his own day, a fallacy that persists in ours as well:

> If, therefore, currency is multiplied, it is a delusion to suppose that capital is multiplied....If banks not only lend capital but also lend "coined credit," some time or other a liquidation must come, there must be an effort to touch the capital which the notes

pretend to convey. Then it is found that they represent nothing; then "credit breaks down," and there must be a settlement, a liquidation, a dividend, and a new start. . . . The real amount of capital we possess is divided up, and we have to make up our minds that we possess only 50 to 75 per cent of what we thought we possessed. We put smaller figures for everything, and reconcile ourselves to smaller hopes, but the experience is soon forgotten, and the old process of inflation and delusion begins again.[17]

The forgotten depression

The often overlooked depression of 1920–1921 is especially instructive for us today. During and after World War I, the Federal Reserve had been inflating the money supply quite substantially, and when it finally began raising the discount rate (the rate at which it lends to banks) the economy slowed as it began its readjustment in line with Austrian business cycle theory.[18] By the middle of 1920 the downturn in production had become severe, falling by 21 percent over the following twelve months. Conditions were worse than they would be in 1930, after the first year of the Great Depression. Yet scarcely any American even knows that such a slowdown occurred. That's probably because, compared to the Great Depression of the 1930s, it was so short lived. Unlike those terrible times, in which the federal government confidently announced its intentions to navigate our way out of it, the market was allowed to make the necessary corrections, and in no time the economy was back to setting production records once again.

Not surprisingly, many modern economists who have studied the depression of 1920–21 have been unable to explain how the recovery could have been so swift and sweeping even though the federal government and the Federal Reserve refrained from employing any of the macroeconomic tools—public works spending, government deficits, inflationary monetary policy—that conventional wisdom recommends as the solutions to economic slowdowns. The Keynesian economist Robert A. Gordon admitted that "government policy to moderate the depression and speed

recovery was minimal. The Federal Reserve authorities were largely pas-
sive.... Despite the absence of a stimulative government policy, however,
recovery was not long delayed."[19] Another economic historian briskly
conceded that "the economy rebounded quickly from the 1920–1921 depression and entered a period of quite vigorous growth," but chose not
to comment on this development, which would appear to fly in the face
of his own preference for monetary and fiscal stimulus.[20]

Compare the U.S. response to that of Japan. In 1920, the Japanese
government introduced the fundamentals of a planned economy, with the
aim of keeping prices artificially high. According to economist Benjamin
Anderson, "The great banks, the concentrated industries, and the government got together, destroyed the freedom of the markets, arrested the
decline in commodity prices, and held the Japanese price level high above
the receding world level for seven years. During these years Japan endured chronic industrial stagnation and at the end, in 1927, she had a
banking crisis of such severity that many great branch bank systems went
down, as well as many industries. It was a stupid policy. In the effort to
avert losses on inventory representing one year's production, Japan lost
seven years."[21]

The U.S., by contrast, allowed its economy to readjust. "In 1920–21,"
says Anderson, "we took our losses, we readjusted our financial structure, we endured our depression, and in August 1921 we started up
again.... The rally in business production and employment that started
in August 1921 was soundly based on a drastic cleaning up of credit
weakness, a drastic reduction in the costs of production, and on the free
play of private enterprise. It was not based on governmental policy designed to make business good." The federal government did not do what
Keynesian economists ever since have urged it to do: run unbalanced
budgets and prime the pump through increased expenditures. Rather,
there prevailed the old-fashioned view that government should keep
spending and taxation low and reduce the public debt.[22]

This episode, since it doesn't fit very neatly into the Official Version
of History™, in which government "stabilization" policies are necessary

to navigate the economy out of the doldrums, is usually passed over in silence.

The groundwork for the Great Depression

This all-too-brief history of boom and bust brings us to the Great Depression. It has never been more important for Americans to understand the background to the Great Depression, and what the government did that made it persist for so long. Fed chairman Ben Bernanke notwithstanding, the Great Depression did not occur because the Fed didn't create enough money. If only the economy were so simple, and prosperity could be restored with a monetary magic wand.[23]

The 1920s have often been thought of as a time of low to nonexistent inflation because consumer prices stayed constant. But in fact the Fed pursued an inflationary policy during the 1920s. The production statistics from 1922 to 1927 show substantial increases in output across major sectors of the economy. Automobile production increased by 4.2 percent per year, petroleum production by 12.6 percent, manufactured goods by four percent, and raw materials at 2.5 percent.[24] With such increase in supply, we should expect prices to fall. They didn't. Why not?

It took a substantial inflation of the money supply just to keep prices stable. And inflation that keeps the price level stable is just as disruptive of the economy's capital structure as one that actually raises consumer prices.[25] Between July 1921 and July 1929 the money supply increased by 55 percent, or by an average annual rate of 7.3 percent.[26] That increase did not take the form of additional currency in circulation (that stayed constant throughout the 1920s). The vast bulk took the form of additional loans to businesses, which is precisely how the increased money supply has to enter the economy for the boom-bust cycle to commence, according to Austrian business cycle theory.[27]

The stock market was especially buoyant during the 1920s, a fact that makes perfect sense in light of the Austrian theory. That theory holds that an inflationary boom will lend an artificial stimulus to capital-goods industries. Since the value of a company's stock represents the value of the company's capital, a stock market bubble is a natural consequence. So is a noticeable stimulus to real estate, the other large market in capital titles.[28]

During the 1920s, economists foolishly assured the American people that permanent prosperity had arrived and that the business cycle had been tamed forever—just as the Great War had ended all wars. Austrian economists earned substantial credibility for themselves by predicting the Great Depression at a time when fashionable opinion held that the boom of the '20s could go on indefinitely. At the same time, Irving Fisher, one of the twentieth century's most celebrated economists and one of the architects of modern mainstream economics, looked at the stable price level and declared that the economy was in excellent shape.

Whoops.

In early September 1929, not two months before the stock market crash, Fisher said: "There may be a recession in stock prices, but not anything in the nature of a crash. Dividend returns on stocks are moving higher. This is not due to receding prices for stocks, and will not be hastened by any anticipated crash, the possibility of which I fail to see."[29]

The next month's worth of predictions is just embarrassing. In mid-October, Fisher declared that stocks had reached a "permanently high plateau," that he expected to see the stock market "a good deal higher than it is today within a few months," and that he did "not feel that there will soon, if ever, be a fifty- or sixty-point break below present levels." The predictions grew even more detached from reality as the month progressed.[30]

The Austrian economist Ludwig von Mises, on the other hand, understood that the inflationary boom was inherently unsustainable and had to come to an end. The permanent prosperity that mainstream economists spoke of was a fantasy, a fraud. "It is clear," said Mises, "that the crisis must come sooner or later. It is also clear that the crisis must always be caused, primarily and directly, by the change in the conduct of the banks. If we speak of error on the part of the banks, however, we must point to the wrong they do in encouraging the upswing. The fault lies, not with the policy of raising the interest rate, but only with the fact that it was raised too late."[31] It was indeed possible to avoid the business cycle, he said, but not through supposedly scientific management of interest rates and the money supply by a central bank like the Fed. Such manipulation and the discoordination in production it caused only sowed the seeds for future business cycles. Central planning, in short, was not the solution. "The only way to do away with, or even to alleviate, the periodic return of the trade cycle—with its denouement, the crisis—is to reject the fallacy that prosperity can be produced by using banking procedures to make credit cheap."[32]

Finally and inevitably, the correction came. The stock market crash of October 1929 was shocking enough, but conditions had grown especially appalling by 1931, which economist Benjamin Anderson called "the tragic year." Sharp declines in output and employment were felt throughout the country.

Hoover was no laissez-faire man—which was exactly the problem

So what did the federal government do? Exactly what Austrian theory suggests it should not do. And instead of a quick liquidation and the return of prosperity, the country suffered economic stagnation for a decade and a half. (And no, World War II didn't end the Depression, either; rationing consumer goods in order to build ships and planes that consumers don't use doesn't create prosperity. More on that below.) Between 1933 and 1940 the unemployment rate averaged 18 percent.

From the point of view of the geniuses at the *Washington Post* and the *New York Times*, this history may as well not have occurred. As our own crisis grew acute in the late summer of 2008, the press was filled with demands for another Franklin D. Roosevelt and another New Deal, so successful had the first one presumably been. On and on it went for weeks on end, as if there were nothing to say against FDR's programs, which have come in for a sober reappraisal in an avalanche of scholarship these writers prefer to ignore. We may presume further that we are not to be so impertinent as to remind our betters at the *Washington Post* that the Great Depression persisted for years and years in the face of the very same interventions they urge upon us now. According to the Official Version of History™, FDR's program pulled the country out of the Depression, no matter what those annoying unemployment figures say.

For decades, American schoolchildren were—and many still are—taught that President Herbert Hoover, who is described as a strict proponent of laissez faire, sat back and did nothing as the Great Depression devastated the country. Only when Franklin Roosevelt took office in March 1933 was serious action taken to arrest the economy's decline. Although most schoolteachers perpetuate this myth even now, it would be considered embarrassing in historical circles to repeat this version of events today.

Hoover expressly said that the laissez-faire approach to the economy was a thing of the past. No peacetime president in American history intervened in the economy to the extent Hoover did. Among other things, he launched public works projects, raised taxes, extended emergency loans to failing firms, hobbled international trade, and lent money to the states for relief programs. He sought to prop up wages at a time when consumer prices were falling dramatically, thereby calling on firms in effect to give raises to their workers at a time of great business vulnerability. This is why Franklin Roosevelt accused Hoover, during the 1932 presidential campaign, of having presided over "the greatest spending administration in peacetime in all of history," and derided him for believing "that we ought to center control of everything in Washington as rapidly as possible." FDR's running mate, John Nance Garner, declared that Hoover was "leading the country down the path to socialism."[33] Meanwhile, the Depression just grew worse and worse.

In 1932, two dozen of the country's leading economists gathered at a conference at the University of Chicago to make recommendations to the federal government. From the point of view of Austrian business cycle theory, the advice they offered to President Hoover was almost uniformly bad, including a more inflationary monetary policy, more subsidies for banks via the Reconstruction Finance Corporation, and a robust program of public works spending—highways, dams, and more.

Two of the participants did offer sound advice, and were of course ignored. One was Gottfried von Haberler, a proponent of Austrian business cycle theory who denounced the "quacks...preaching inflationary measures." The other voice of sense was H. Parker Willis, a Columbia University professor of economics and former editor of the *Journal of Commerce* who warned that further inflation of the money supply would only intensify existing resource misallocation. "Any such step at the present time," he explained, "would simply mean an aggravation of existing difficulties, due to the fact that we are already overburdened with construction work and fixed capital that are not likely soon to be employed."[34] As usual, the quacks prevailed.

How FDR made it persist

When FDR took office he did indeed make much bolder moves than his predecessor, but even Rexford Tugwell, one of his key advisers, later admitted that much of what constituted FDR's New Deal programs was just a series of extrapolations from what Hoover had already been doing. FDR took Hoover's efforts to prop up prices and wages and institutionalized them. He mistakenly believed falling prices had been a *cause* of the Depression (they were a consequence, not a cause), so he thought keeping prices high was the way to prosperity.[35] Hoover's agricultural policy had aimed at increasing farm prices; FDR now did so through destroying existing crops and imposing acreage reduction requirements on farmers. FDR signed legislation suspending the antitrust rules so industries could organize themselves into cartels that would establish minimum selling prices, limit output, and impose other restrictions on free economic activity. He raised taxes still more, expanded public works spending, and established federal welfare programs.

In short, the Hoover-Roosevelt program refused to allow the economy's bubble to deflate. It tried to prop up unsound business positions. It diverted capital from a private sector starved for real savings into uneconomic public works projects that contributed nothing to long-term economic adjustment. It interfered with the free movement of prices and wages, thereby obstructing the economy's attempt to reallocate resources according to genuine consumer preferences and to reestablish a sustainable level of prices. And everyone professed to be mystified that the awaited economic correction, which the government hadn't *allowed* to occur, hadn't occurred.

One economist correctly observed in the early 1930s:

> Nobody wishes for bankruptcies. Nobody likes liquidation as such. If bankruptcy and liquidation can be avoided by sound financing nobody would be against such measures. All that is contended is that when the extent of malinvestment and overindebtedness has passed a certain limit, measures which postpone liquidation only tend to make matters worse. No doubt in the first years of depression, to those who held short views of the disturbance, anything seemed preferable to a smash. But is it really clear, in the fourth year of depression, that a more astringent policy in 1930 would have been likely to cause more disturbance and dislocation than the dislocation and disturbance which have actually been caused by its postponement?[36]

Although much of it is collecting dust on the shelves, a substantial literature exists that gives a non-fantasy view of the consequences of the New Deal. Two UCLA economists, for instance, showed in the *Journal of Political Economy* in 2004 that the Depression lasted so long not *in spite* of FDR's New Deal programs but *because* of them. "New Deal labor and industrial policies did not lift the economy out of the Depression as President Roosevelt had hoped," wrote Harold Cole and Lee Ohanian. "The subsequent abandonment of these policies coincided with the strong economic recovery of the 1940s."[37]

It has been argued that the Depression was so severe because the money supply was too low. A closer look suggests the problem was government interference with the price system. Consider: the money supply decreased in practically the same proportions during the years 1839–1843 as in 1929–1933. In the earlier case, government allowed prices to fall freely. The data show a 21 percent increase in real consumption and a 16 percent increase in real GNP during those years. Investment did fall by 23 percent, not surprisingly for a period of economic correction in the wake of malinvestments encouraged in a preceding boom. In the period from 1929 to 1933, on the other hand, in which the federal government artificially propped up prices and wages, the result was a decline in real consumption of 19 percent, a 30 percent drop in GNP, and a 91 percent decrease in real gross investment.[38]

Did we spend our way out of the Depression?

Predictably enough, the usual reply to the argument that the New Deal failed to lift the country out of the Depression is to claim that government spending hadn't been quite high enough in the 1930s, and that if still more resources could have been seized from the private economy and spent on arbitrary projects, prosperity would have been restored.

To this day, some Keynesians try to argue further that the sharp downturn of 1937–38, a kind of depression within the depression, was caused by the federal government's decision to run lower budget deficits and its supposedly insufficient public-works spending. Conspicuously absent from this account is the fact that money wages skyrocketed by 13.7 percent in the first three quarters of 1937, thanks to increased labor union activity resulting from the Supreme Court's favorable decision on the National Labor Relations Act of 1935. This spurt in wage rates did not reflect an increase in productivity, and was far out of proportion to any rise in output prices. Naturally, employment declined and economic activity slowed as a result. Increased labor costs associated with various social welfare programs only aggravated the problem. In short, we need not be detained by the claim that insufficient government spending was the culprit behind the economic woes of those years.[39]

According to Paul Krugman, "What saved the economy, and the New Deal, was the enormous public works project known as World War II, which finally provided a fiscal stimulus adequate to the economy's needs."[40]

This stupefying and bizarre misunderstanding of what actually happened needs to be debunked, because so many proposals today are based on the same foolish idea that as long as government spending and indebtedness are great enough, prosperity will follow.

Is there any truth to the notion that World War II stimulated the American economy? Unemployment did fall substantially during the war, it is true, but presumably we can figure out without too much mental effort what happens to unemployment when 29 percent of the prewar labor force is at one time or another drafted into the armed forces.

Economic historian Robert Higgs, in a couple of articles that appeared in professional journals in the 1990s, made the most effective assault on the hoary old myth of wartime prosperity. By the time Oxford University Press published his *Depression, War, and Cold War* in 2006, Higgs' thesis was even beginning to find its way into the textbooks. Higgs urges us to consider the sudden and severe resource constraints that afflicted the American economy during those years. With 29 percent of the labor force shifted into the armed forces at some point during the war, their places were taken by elderly men and by women and teenagers with relatively little work experience. We are supposed to believe that an economy suffering from these disabilities somehow managed to achieve average real GDP growth rates of 13 percent per year, an achievement never matched in American history before or since? And we're also supposed to believe that when the original labor force was restored at the end of the war, the American economy's real output would *fall* by 22 percent over the next two years?

It does not speak well for mainstream economics that so many of its students believed such obvious nonsense for so long. These conclusions come directly from what the statistics tell us, a critic may object. Well, might there be something a little fishy about those statistics, given that they lead us to absurd conclusions?

The problem is that the national income statistics gathered during the war are meaningless. For reasons we'll see in chapter 6, Gross Domestic Product is an aggregate of dubious value even under ideal circumstances. But during the war the national income statistics were more misleading than usual. Only the free interaction of buyers and sellers, of demand and supply, can give rise to meaningful prices on the free market. If the government were to claim, unilaterally and in isolation from market exchange, "From now on, the price of eggs will be $10 apiece, and we'll be ordering one million of them," how would our understanding of real conditions in the economy be enhanced by multiplying the arbitrary price of $10 by one million eggs, arriving at $10 million, and adding that to our national income?

But that's in effect what happened during the war. With at least two-fifths of national output now part of the war machine, with large portions of the remainder under various kinds of controls and with spillover effects throughout the economy, the price system became more and more arbitrary. Prices arose not out of the free interaction of buyers and sellers. They were arbitrarily imposed by government and did not reflect consumer choice. Adding up a bunch arbitrary numbers yields nothing but a great big arbitrary number. But it's those numbers, the GDP figures during the war, on which the tall tale of wartime prosperity is based.[41]

In the midst of all this, consumers also had to suffer rationing, declining product quality, the complete inability to purchase things like new homes, cars, and appliances, and an increase in the work week. How significant is a "boom" in which consumer welfare is subject to constraints like this? But there's your big prosperity.

Oh, and we were warned that with the war over, the boys coming home and military spending slashed, the country would plunge into the doldrums again. Exactly the opposite happened, of course: 1946 was a year of fantastic prosperity, in which the private sector experienced the single greatest growth spurt in American history. This is a big mystery to a certain school of economists, but common sense to everyone else: when your economy shifts back to producing things consumers need and its labor force is increased and improved, the economy improves.

The national income accounting statistics showed a great decline in American prosperity in 1946—another absurdity—though if we take bad economists' advice and accept the wartime statistics at face value, then we must also take at face value the same statistical aggregates when they tell us the economy tanked in 1946. The health of the *private economy*, which is where wealth is generated, was very poor during the war and excellent afterward. This is really just common sense (but if it weren't for the denial of common sense, most of our public intellectuals would have nothing to do).

If spending on munitions really makes a country wealthy, the United States and Japan should do the following:

Each should seek to build the most spectacular naval fleet in history, an enormous armada of gigantic, powerful, technologically advanced ships. The two fleets should then meet in the Pacific. Naturally, since they would want to avoid the loss of life that accompanies war, all naval personnel would be evacuated from the ships. At that point the U.S. and Japan would sink each other's fleets. Then they could celebrate how much richer they had made themselves by devoting labor, steel, and countless other inputs to the production of things that would wind up at the bottom of the ocean.[42]

We have dwelled on the "war brings prosperity" argument because it is based on the same central fallacy as the "consumer spending drives the economy" silliness, which we'll encounter in chapter 6, and because it is believed by the great majority of the geniuses who presume to offer us advice now.

Both of these fallacies assume that the mere act of spending, regardless of what the money is spent on, gives rise to prosperity. It's good for the economy, they tell us, if people empty their pockets during a recession, even though that's the opposite of what a sensible person would do. We're also told that if government spends feverishly on things consumers don't buy and can't use (like fighter planes and tanks, for instance), and then taxes the private economy or borrows in order to pay for it, it thereby makes everyone richer. That is the philosophy behind fiscal "stimulus" programs as well. Anyone who buys an absurdity like this belongs in a lunatic asylum, or on the editorial page of the *New York Times*. Ludwig von Mises had it right: "War prosperity is like the prosperity that an earthquake or a plague brings."

Lessons for today

The parallel between the Great Depression and the current crisis is not exact, but enough similarities exist between the two episodes to make the comparison worthwhile. In both cases, an inflationary credit boom brought about by the Fed's lowering of interest rates led to massive resource misallocation and a distorted capital structure. The Fed tried in vain to inflate each of these booms back into existence, and grew frustrated with banks that refused to lend out the new money it was pumping into the banking system. In both cases the federal government sought to prop up prices—commodity prices and consumer prices in the Great Depression, and asset prices today—rather than allowing them to fall to a level that made sense in light of economic conditions and people's valuations of the goods and assets in question. In both cases short-selling was attacked, speculators condemned, and salvation sought in public works programs and government pump-priming. Emergency lending was extended to firms in trouble.

If we want a repeat of those years, or if we'd like to share the fate of Japan for the past 18 years, we should listen to Paul Krugman and implement exactly the same policies that gave the world these two disasters. On the other hand, we might for once permit ourselves a heretical deviation from the Official Version of History™, cease waving incense before the Great Presidents we are taught to admire, and consider the possibility that the government's efforts to fight depressions may in fact have lengthened them. Let's spare ourselves the ordeal of a ten-year depression—and the added indignity of being told ten years from now that it was the government's brilliant plan that eventually rescued us.

CHAPTER 6

MONEY

If there's one issue that fashionable opinion doesn't want discussed in connection with the economic crisis, it's money. Specifically, there are certain things we're not supposed to wonder about, including points that this book has implicitly or explicitly raised:

- Whether a system that has caused the dollar to lose 95 percent of its value is really the best of all possible systems
- Whether it's desirable for government to be able to create out of thin air however much money it needs—thereby enabling it to avoid the more obvious routes of taxation and borrowing, and instead expropriate the people less conspicuously
- Whether a system in which government cannot manipulate the money supply and artificially push down interest rates (thereby giving rise to the boom-bust cycle) might be more stable than the one we have now

- Whether another kind of monetary system might make it harder for government to bail out its friends—even refusing to disclose who is getting what—in defiance of popular opposition
- Whether another kind of monetary system might discourage the reckless leveraging and risk-taking that has flourished under the present system[1]

To read *Newsweek* and the *New York Times* or listen to the financial commentators on television, you'd never get the sense that our monetary system itself might have something to do with the current crisis. Now nobody likes to consider the awful possibility that *Newsweek* and the *Times* could actually be overlooking something, but circumstances have forced us to that sad conclusion.

The reader should infer from this book's argument that the system of money and banking we now have—including the central bank—is a source of economic instability and miscalculation. We need to consider alternatives to it. Virtually all analysis of the economy today, on the other hand, takes for granted that regulatory tinkering is all that is needed to patch up an otherwise sound monetary system.

To the contrary: *the system itself is the problem*, and the sooner we cast away the foolish web of superstitions that stand in the way of serious, productive discussion of the issue, the better off the American people will be.

If we expect to find the answers to our economic woes and instability by looking only at the surface, we are going to be disappointed. For once, we need to ask some fundamental questions, whether or not they happen to be the ones that fashionable opinion is asking. The purpose of this chapter is to introduce some important concepts and to overturn some of the myths that stand in the way of evaluating the idea of getting government out of the money business.

Where does money come from?

Where does money come from in the first place? It doesn't originate with government. Money originally came about because people grew dissatisfied with barter, the primitive system in which goods are exchanged *directly* for one another: basketballs for hats, history lectures for newspapers. Since people who own basketballs don't necessarily wish to exchange them for hats, and most newspaper vendors are not looking to unload their wares in order to hear someone speak about the War of 1812, this system is unsatisfactory. (It is unsatisfactory for many other reasons, too: how, for instance, does someone whose only possession is a castle buy a loaf of bread?)

A money economy, unlike barter, is one in which goods are exchanged *indirectly* for each other: instead of having to be a hat-wanting basketball owner in the possibly vain search for a basketball-wanting hat owner, the basketball owner instead exchanges his basketball for whatever is functioning as money—let's say gold or silver—and then exchanges the gold or silver for the hat he wants.

Here we reach the origin of money. People who are dissatisfied with the clumsy system of barter perceive that if they can acquire a more widely desired (and therefore more marketable) good than the one they currently possess, they are more likely to find someone willing to exchange with them. That more widely desired good can be anything from berries to shells to gold, all of which have served this purpose in various historical cases. And the more that good begins to be used as a common medium of exchange, the more people who have no particular desire for it in and of itself will be eager to acquire it anyway, because they know other people will accept it in exchange for goods. Even if you have no direct use for a precious metal, you will still want to acquire it because you know you can make exchanges with it. In that way, gold and silver (or whatever else the money happens to be) evolve into full-fledged media of exchange, or money.

Money, therefore, comes about spontaneously as a useful commodity on the market. It is not arbitrarily introduced by government decree. Nor could it be. For one thing, who would go along with the idea without having experienced it first? As economist Robert Murphy puts it, only a genius could have envisioned money and its possibilities without having observed it, and he would have sounded like a crank if he tried to describe it. ("Instead of trading away your valuable pigs for horses, why not accept some smooth stones? Don't worry that you don't want them; someone else will give you those horses in exchange for the stones! C'mon, everybody, if we could all just agree that these useful stones are valuable, we'd all be so much better off!")[2]

Also, a money has to originate on the market in this way, since only then would people know what its value was. In the process of becoming a money, it would acquire an array of prices of other goods in terms of itself. Only with this pre-existing array of barter prices could people use the money. If it were just forced on the people out of nowhere, the public would have no way of assessing its value, and it would be useless to them. A paper money, therefore, *cannot* originate from a simple government decree. It has to have a link to a money that society had spontaneously adopted in the (however distant) past. Even the notorious paper monies of the American and French Revolutions were initially defined in terms of an existing commodity money, and then depreciated from there.

Enter government

In other words, fiat paper money is always parasitic on a previously existing commodity money, and could not come about without it.* The usual pattern runs as follows: (1) society adopts a commodity money; (2) paper notes issued by banks (or by governments) that can be redeemed in a given weight of the commodity money begin to circulate as a convenient substitute for carrying precious metal coins; and (3) government

---

*A commodity money is a medium of exchange that either is a commercial commodity (like gold or silver) or that represents title to such a commodity. Paper money can be used in such a system, but the paper would be redeemable into the commodity itself. The paper would not be the money; the paper is merely a convenient substitute for the money, which would be gold, silver, or whatever the commodity was. A fiat money is a medium of exchange that is not a commodity or a producer or consumer good, and does not represent title to such a good. It is paper that is redeemable into nothing. That is the system we have now.

confiscates the commodity to which the paper notes entitle their holders, and thereby leaves the people with an inconvertible fiat paper money.[3]

The substitution of fiat paper money for an existing commodity money always and everywhere comes about by some government violation of private property rights. It always involves the threat of violence and never occurs voluntarily.[4] After 1933, when the federal government ordered Americans to hand over all their monetary gold to the authorities, the paper money that had once been a claim to a weight of gold continued to circulate out of habit, and because an array of prices had already come into existence in terms of that money.

Over the course of history, societies have most often chosen gold and silver as money. Soon enough, governments decided they wanted a piece of the action, and kings and other rulers began to stamp their faces on the coins and monopolize the production of money. This, their people were led to understand, was a rightful attribute of sovereignty to which their leaders were entitled. Public-good rationales notwithstanding, what government monopolies on money production actually meant was that the ruler could now loot the population by clipping the coins and debasing the currency, inserting some amount of base metal into previously pure coins and pocketing the difference himself.

Moralists, theologians, and other intellectuals condemned such behavior. In the fourteenth century, for instance, Nicholas Oresme (c. 1323–82), bishop and scientist, composed *A Treatise on the Origin, Nature, Law, and Alterations of Money*, which analyzed inflation as an economic problem and sharply criticized the practice on moral and economic grounds. Juan de Mariana (1536–1624) wrote a devastating treatise (*De mutatione monetae*) against monetary debasement, condemning it as a kind of theft. This, of course, was before rulers could rely on compliant economists to assure everyone that debasing money promoted economic growth, and that it wasn't really debasement anyway: it was just making the money more *flexible*.

Paper money suited governments rather better than coins of precious metal, since they could enrich themselves and their friends without arousing the suspicions and public hostility that debasing coins provoked. All they needed to do was print up additional paper money and spend it. It was also easier to blame scapegoats—wicked businessmen, speculators, and the rest of the rogues' gallery of people the population is taught to hate— for the rising prices that paper-money inflation caused.

Why gold and silver?

All kinds of commodities have served as monies throughout history, but precious metals like gold and silver have been the most common. These metals are durable, easily divisible, and relatively valuable per unit weight. Gold is so valuable, in fact, that gold coins are not usually convenient for the kinds of transactions people normally make every day. That's why silver coins are generally used for smaller transactions, with copper coins sometimes used for even smaller ones.

Governments tend to oppose monetary systems based on precious metals because they impose restraints on ambitious politicians. Gold cannot be infinitely reproduced, as can paper money. Even if paper money is used under a commodity standard, the paper is a money substitute that can be converted into the commodity whenever people demand it. If governments try to print paper money beyond the gold or silver they possess, their scheme will collapse as soon as people take that paper and demand the money commodity for it. Government can be stymied in its money creation by the people's redemption claims of paper into precious metal. Not surprisingly, government prefers a system in which the paper money cannot be redeemed into anything. Then it can increase the supply of money without restraint.

Unable to print all the money it wants, government under a commodity standard must resort to borrowing or taxation, both of which are more obvious and meet with sterner resistance than the silent means of inflation. W. Randolph Burgess, chairman of the executive committee of the National City Bank of New York, told a meeting of the American Bankers Association in 1949:

Historically one of the best protections of the value of money against the inroads of political spending was the gold standard—the redemption of money in gold on demand. This put a check-rein on the politician. For inflationary spending led to the loss of gold either by exports or by withdrawals by individuals who distrusted government policies. This was a kind of automatic limit on credit expansion. . . .

Of course the modern economic planners don't like the gold standard just because it does put a limit on their powers. . . . I have great confidence that the world will return to the gold standard in some form because the people in so many countries have learned that they need protection from the excesses of their political leaders. . . . [5]

As we'll see, the economic arguments against a commodity money are little more than a string of fallacies. But Joseph Schumpeter, one of the twentieth century's great economists, argued that even if someone were to accept all the misplaced economic arguments against gold, it still made sense to favor a gold standard, because a commodity standard was the only monetary system compatible with freedom. Writing in the early 1950s, Schumpeter observed that people had been taught to look upon the idea of the gold standard as

wholly erroneous—as a sort of fetishism that is impervious to rational argument. We are also taught to discount all rational and all purely economic arguments that may actually be adduced in favor of it. But quite irrespective of these, there is one point about the gold standard that would redeem it from the charge of foolishness; even in the absence of any purely economic advantage. . . . An automatic gold currency is part and parcel of a laissez-faire and free-trade economy. . . . *This* is the reason why gold is so unpopular now and also why it was so popular in the bourgeois era.

It imposes restrictions upon governments or bureaucracies that
are much more powerful than is parliamentary criticism. It is both
the badge and the guarantee of bourgeois freedom—of freedom
not simply of the bourgeois *interest*, but of freedom in the bourgeois *sense*. From this standpoint *a man may quite rationally fight
for it, even if fully convinced of the validity of all that has ever
been urged against it on economic grounds*.[6]

Concerned about theft, consumers under a commodity standard often
prefer to store their precious metals for safekeeping at what might be
called a money warehouse. In exchange for their silver (or whatever the
money commodity happens to be) they receive a warehouse receipt,
which they present at the money warehouse, or bank, whenever they
wish to reclaim their property. If the warehouse keeper has a reputation
for honesty, his customers will often be happy to use the warehouse receipts themselves as a more convenient method of making purchases,
knowing that these pieces of paper are claims to real silver that can be
redeemed on demand. These warehouse receipts thus evolve into what
are eventually called bank notes. These bank notes are money substitutes,
or claims to real money (in this case, the silver in the vault).[7]

Eventually, the warehouse keeper realizes that since people trust that
his paper notes can be instantly redeemed for silver, only a very small
fraction of the silver he has in his vault is ever actually demanded by depositors. In other words, since they know they *can* get their silver if they
want it, they rarely bother to do so. The paper notes that represent the
silver work just fine to facilitate their transactions. The warehouse
keeper, in turn, becomes confident that he can meet all of the relatively
small number of redemption demands of paper notes into silver even if
he lends out as interest-earning loans a large fraction of the silver in his
vault. He will therefore have more notes (or, as the system grows more
sophisticated, checking deposits) in circulation than he has units of silver
in his vault to correspond to them. This is "fractional reserve" banking,
since the bank keeps on reserve only a fraction of the funds depositors

have entrusted to it, lending out the rest to borrowers. If absolutely everyone, or even just a substantial portion, of the people who had stored their silver with him should come claiming it at the same time, he would be unable to honor their redemption requests and would have to go out of business. But since such swarms of simultaneous demands never seem to occur, he feels safe enough pursuing this strategy.[8]

A "bank run" occurs when depositors, having lost confidence in the soundness of their bank, flock to the bank to withdraw their funds out of a concern that not all of the bank's clients will be able to retrieve their money. The individuals involved just want to gain possession of their own property, but both in the present and throughout history it is they, rather than the banks that cannot produce their clients' property, who are condemned as selfish, anti-social, and unpatriotic. (Time deposits are another matter—in that case, a depositor expressly agrees that for a specified period of time he will be able to access his money only with a penalty, if at all. Banks can lend *these* funds without fear of a run, for as long as the loans they make are repaid before their own depositors' instruments reach maturity, they will have enough funds on hand to satisfy their clients' claims.)

A central bank like the Fed can coordinate the banks' creation of new money so that the entire banking system inflates together. The Fed's creation of new money increases the reserves of the banking system as a whole, and since the banks, seeking profit, will lend out as great a percentage of this new money as the law allows them to, they will all tend to create new money on the basis of these Fed injections at the same rate.* The banks can't just print up more notes, since the Fed has a monopoly on that, but they can make loans in the form of checking deposits created out of thin air. (If borrowers should want to convert these checking

---

*Namely, the maximum rate the reserve requirement allows. The reserve requirement, as its name indicates, is the percentage of deposits that the central bank requires its member banks to keep on reserve in order to satisfy day-to-day customer demands for cash.

deposits into cash, the bank draws down its account with the Fed to satisfy this demand.) With all banks expanding the supply of money at the
same rate, the various redemptions (of checks from one bank for cash at
another, for example) will tend on net to cancel each other out. Banks
could get into trouble if they tried to inflate *beyond* the rate the Fed
wants, to be sure, though even here they can have recourse to the federal
funds market, in which banks that happen to have surplus reserves can
lend to banks having short-term difficulties. In extreme cases, the Fed has
the power to act as "lender of last resort," supplying additional reserves
to troubled banks or buying assets from them.

Banks are still liable to runs, but the very existence of the central
bank, along with so-called deposit insurance, makes them much less
likely—not only because these institutions stand ready to bail out the
banks, but also because they give the public a misleading impression of
their soundness. As a result, there is much less turnover in the banking
industry, and the same people pursuing the same financial strategies and
practices tend to persist and become entrenched to a far greater degree
than they would under a system of genuine competition.[9]

In the United States, the Panic of 1907, which involved banks that
could not meet their obligations to depositors, gave important impetus
to an already-existing movement to establish a central bank. On October 21, 1907, there was a run on the Knickerbocker Trust Company in
New York that caused that bank to fail. Three days later, the city's
second-largest trust company also experienced a run. Concerned that
their deposits were not being safely cared for by the banks, people began
demanding currency at banks all over the country. The banks could not
honor their depositors' requests for cash, because instead of keeping it
available on demand they were holding it in income-earning securities.
Should they engage in a massive sale of these securities in order to satisfy
depositors' demand for cash, the prices of those securities would be
driven down and the banks' assets would be degraded.[10]

Economist Gene Smiley, reflecting on what happened in 1907, explains that "there was no 'lender of last resort,' or bankers' bank, in the

United States that could make loans to the banks themselves when banks required additional currency. And by the early twentieth century there began to be a need for such an institution."[11] Smiley himself is a free-market economist in everything but money, so he is not naturally given to government solutions, but notice how readily the basic question is begged: there began to be a "need" for an institution that could rescue banks that got into trouble when they could not produce their clients' money on demand. Is it really so unthinkable that the banks should not be playing fast and loose with their depositors' money in the first place? We might just as readily say there was a "need" to force them to behave honestly or be forced to close their doors. So entrenched is the bailout mentality when it comes to the financial sector that such an option is never even raised.[12]

The Federal Reserve System

The Federal Reserve System, like all institutions of long standing, benefits from an intellectual inertia that discourages inquiry, including the very idea that an institution like the Fed might be something worth inquiring about. Even—or perhaps especially—those who claim to live by the motto "question authority" fall silent when it comes to the Fed. Feeding into this inertia is the naïve, civics-textbook model of government that most Americans have absorbed from elementary school. The naïve view, as applied to the Fed, is that when the American people spontaneously cried out for banking reform, their public-spirited representatives, eager to pursue the common good, sprang to action and devised wise and appropriate legislation. The result was an institution that managed the monetary system in the interest of all, and informed by the best and soundest economic science of the day.

Nothing in the above scenario is true, but to the extent that most Americans give any thought to the Fed at all, that seems to be roughly how they assume it must have come about. In fact, as with so much of what is signed into law, the Federal Reserve Act of 1913 was special-interest legislation masquerading as a public-spirited measure. The truth of the matter, that bankers themselves drafted the Federal Reserve Act in a private meeting in Jekyll Island, Georgia, in 1910, almost sounds too kooky and bizarre to take seriously. Now we can either believe that this is the first and only time in history in which an interest group drafted legislation aimed more at the public good than their own benefit, or we can consider the possibility that its intent was to entrench special privileges for one particular industry at the expense of the rest of society. Oddly enough, the very people who are normally willing to entertain the basest motives for anything bankers and businessmen do are the ones least likely to suspect that the Fed itself might have been the product of special-interest thinking.

The Federal Reserve controls the American money supply and can influence interest rates either upward or downward; it can also function as a "lender of last resort." Although people use the phrase "printing money" as a kind of shorthand for what the Fed does, the Fed increases the money supply not by printing cash and putting it into circulation, but by what are called "open-market operations," which involve the purchase and sale of assets.[13] Strictly speaking, the Fed can purchase any kind of asset it wants, but it normally purchases government bonds. If it wants to increase the money supply, it purchases, say, $1 billion in bonds from a bond dealer. It makes the purchase by writing a check on itself for $1 billion and handing it to a firm like Goldman Sachs in exchange for the bonds. It creates this $1 billion out of thin air.

Goldman Sachs then deposits this $1 billion check from the Fed in its bank. That bank doesn't put the $1 billion in a special vault with "Goldman's Money" on the door. Instead, the bank will lend out most of that $1 billion, since the law only requires it to keep a small percentage of its deposits on reserve. (Most of the bank's reserves, incidentally, are kept in its own account at the Fed, with a small amount in cash in its vaults to satisfy normal day-to-day requests for cash by the bank's depositors.) When the bank, in turn, lends out the money, borrowers spend it, and it winds up in accounts in other banks, which use most of that money in still another round of expansion, and so on. With a reserve requirement of ten percent, the initial $1 billion will have supported $9 billion in additional lending by the time this process is complete. All of this $10 billion has been created out of nothing: the initial $1 billion check from the Fed, and the additional $9 billion in loans that fractional-reserve banking makes possible, were produced out of thin air. Should the Fed wish to contract credit, it follows this procedure in reverse: it *sells* bonds to the banks, and the money it receives for them—and the further increase in the money supply that the fractional-reserve system then created on top of it—are withdrawn from the economy.[14]

The Fed has other mechanisms available to control the money supply. One is to raise or lower the discount rate, which is the rate at which the Fed itself extends loans to banks. It can also change the banks' reserve requirements, which means it can tell the banks they need to keep five, ten, twenty, or whatever percent of its deposits on reserve rather than lent out. Obviously, the lower the reserve requirement, the more money the bank can lend and the greater the multiplication effect we saw above.

What is inflation, and why is it bad?

Although people often define inflation as a general rise in prices, and economists themselves employ that definition as a kind of shorthand, inflation is actually the increase of the money supply itself (which in turn *leads to* higher prices than would otherwise have prevailed). Specifically, it is an increase in the amount of money in circulation not backed by the monetary commodity—in other words, an increase in paper-note claims to gold not backed by increases in gold itself. Under a fiat standard, which the countries of the world have now, in which the monetary system is not backed by a commodity, we can define inflation simply as an increase in the amount of paper money in circulation.[15]

Thus the higher prices that people describe as "inflation" are not themselves the inflation; they are a *consequence* of the increase in (or inflation of) the money supply. Inflation always applies an upward pressure on prices—when more money is chasing an unchanged supply of goods, buyers are able and willing to pay more for them, giving sellers in turn the ability to charge more. But sometimes inflation can occur without rising prices—if, for example, an increased abundance of goods had been pushing prices lower, a greater money supply, by putting *upward* pressure on prices, could cancel out that downward trend and keep the overall price level stable. People wouldn't notice any price increases, but inflation of the money supply would have occurred all the same. In that case, the inflation deprives us of the increases in our standard of living that falling prices would have brought about.

One of the most common complaints about inflation is that it hurts people on fixed incomes: the prices for the goods they buy go up while their incomes stay the same. This is bad enough, but the problems of inflation go well beyond this effect of a steadily rising level of consumer prices.

Consider this question: in what order and in what way does the new money make its way through the economy? When the government inflates the money supply, the new money does not reach everyone simultaneously and proportionately. It enters the economy at discrete points. The earliest recipients of the new money include politically favored constituencies of one kind or another: banks, for example, or firms with government contracts—in other words, wherever government spends money. These privileged parties receive the new money *before* inflation has pushed prices upwards. In effect the economy doesn't yet know how much the money supply has increased, and prices have not yet adjusted accordingly. By the time the new money makes its way through the whole economy, prices will have risen throughout practically all sectors. But *while* this process is taking place, the privileged firms that are lucky enough to get the new money early benefit from being able to make their purchases at the previously existing price level—thereby silently looting those from whom they buy. When the average person gets his hands on this new money—through higher wages, say, or lower borrowing costs—prices have already been rising for quite a while, and he's been paying those prices all this time on his existing income. The value of his money was diluted by the new money before it ever reached him.

Here is another way to think about it: Money in your possession is compensation for some good or service you have provided. When you buy a dozen apples, you do so with the proceeds from a good or service that you yourself provided in the past. So you are able to buy those apples because in the past you provided someone else with something he needed.

Now imagine a situation in which business firms or banks connected to the government receive a new influx of money courtesy of Fed credit expansion. That money comes out of thin air, not from the sale of some previous good or service. Thus when these favored firms spend this money, they are in effect taking goods out of the economy *without providing anything themselves.* Here we see very clearly how they benefit at the expense of the rest of society: they take from the stock of goods without giving anything in return. The money they pay for their goods didn't originate in a good or service that they themselves had previously provided; it came from nowhere. The analogous case under a system of barter would be one in which, instead of trading my bread for your orange juice, I just take your orange juice.

Another problem is that inflation discourages saving. If people know their money will be worth less over time, they have a greater incentive to spend it right away rather than save it and watch its purchasing power decline. The old-fashioned virtue of thrift is thereby scorned and disdained, and immediate gratification encouraged. Hyperinflation, the most extreme form of inflation, illustrates this point most vividly, encouraging immediate consumption on whatever goods are available. When the public realizes that the monetary authority intends to continue inflating the money supply and thus reducing its value, they scramble to unload their currency before it can lose any more purchasing power. In what is called the "flight into real values," consumers seek to abandon their currency at all costs, exchanging it for whatever goods they can find. Only a fool would want to save his money during a hyperinflation that threatens to rob that money of all its value. But this is only an extraordinary case of the more general principle that inflation discourages saving.

Before the advent of paper money backed by nothing, people could save for the future and for their old age simply by accumulating and saving some of the gold and silver coins that then functioned as money. Those coins either maintained or increased their value with the passage of time since their quantity remained relatively stable, while the array of goods in the economy that they could be exchanged for was consistently rising. Today, on the other hand, with unbacked paper money losing value all the time, only a fool would save for his retirement by piling up stacks of Federal Reserve notes (i.e., dollar bills). To try to keep ahead of inflation he is forced to enter the financial markets, where he has to make difficult and risky decisions about what to do with his money in order to stop his retirement nest egg from losing value before his eyes.[16]

We have already seen some of the other outcomes of the Fed's increase of the money supply (by purchasing government bonds and thus adding to banks' reserves), including an increase in risky behavior, a lowering of lending standards, and the business cycle itself. After encouraging all these things and severely disrupting the economy, the Fed then has the power to disrupt it further by bailing out the most irresponsible parties. "Paper money producers," writes a monetary economist, "have an almost unlimited ability to bail out any market participant. This entails the problem known as 'moral hazard'—market participants with good personal and professional connections to the paper money producer invest in excessively risky ventures. When these investments turn sour, the paper money producer bails them out."[17]

Every one of the problems described in this section can be avoided with a commodity money like gold or silver, whose supply is not nearly so easy to increase as paper money. But the possibility of returning to a commodity money is so far from the table that our talking heads have decided it is not even to be mentioned, except perhaps for purposes of ridicule. Meanwhile, the problems created by government's monopoly powers and its central bank's manipulation of money and interest rates are, hilariously enough, blamed on the "free market."

What causes price inflation?

As we've seen, rising prices are one of the consequences of an increase in the money supply. The more money that is created, the less any one unit of money is worth, and therefore the more units of money will be necessary to purchase any given bundle of goods. But politicians always try to persuade us that some dastardly villain—not the government—is driving up prices.

Governments have traditionally blamed rising prices on innocent parties whose unpopularity made them effective scapegoats. Thus for years price inflation was blamed on labor unions, greedy businessmen, "speculators," and the like. Such crude arguments are heard less often today. Nevertheless, there is no shortage of explanations for inflation, such as rising oil prices or an "overheating economy."

Many Americans probably believe phenomena like high oil prices cause inflation. Since gasoline is so central to the economy, the argument goes, and gasoline is an input in so many production processes (as well as in the transportation of goods), any rises in its price will put pressure on many if not all other prices.

In fact, though, high oil prices cannot cause overall price inflation. If the price of a gallon of gas increases, people may indeed spend more of their incomes on gas than they used to. But that means they will have *less* income to spend on all goods *other than gas*. This is the essential fallacy in all "cost-push" accounts of inflation, which try to blame increases in the *overall* price level on increases in *individual* prices like oil. The decreased amount of money people have to spend on goods other than gas puts offsetting *downward pressure* on the prices of all those other goods. So although *gas prices* may rise (and may in turn trigger price increases in certain goods that are sensitive to gas prices but for which demand is inelastic), people will have less money left over to buy all other goods, and the demand for—and thus the price of—those other goods will fall. There is no *overall* increase in the price level.*

The only way all prices can rise simultaneously, apart from a decrease in the supply of all goods (an extremely rare occurrence), is if the amount of money in the economy increases. Only in that case could the American people as a whole spend more on gas *and* more on all other things, such that their added expenditure on gas would not require them to cut back on their purchases of everything else. If they spend more on gas and more on other things, the additional economy-wide spending will indeed make the overall price level rise. Under our fiat system, the money supply can be increased only by the Federal Reserve. The Fed is, for that reason, exclusively responsible for price inflation.

"The Fed should inject credit!"

So the Fed has the power to increase the supply of money in the banking system, with that quantity subsequently multiplied many times over by means of the fractional-reserve principle. The more money it creates, the more lending the banks can do. Not surprisingly, we hear pleas all the time for the Fed to inject credit into the economy in this way. *We need the Fed to push down rates so there can be more borrowing and lending. Then we'll be prosperous.* Such advice is everywhere: we hear it from politicians, the media (even, to their everlasting shame, the business media), and pundits left and right alike.

It is one of the great economic superstitions of our time.

---

*Some have tried to argue that credit cards validate the cost-push approach, since widely available credit makes it possible in our gasoline example for people indeed to spend more on gas and more on other goods at the same time. In an economy based on sound money, though, any extension of credit must be preceded by an act of saving. Nothing can be lent that is not first saved. And so any additional spending that credit makes possible is the counterpart of someone else's equivalent abstention from spending. So no overall rise in prices can be brought about by credit cards, either.

Imagine Robinson Crusoe living in isolation on his island. He decides one day that if he fashioned a net to catch fish he would be more efficient than if he kept trying to catch them with his bare hands. Suppose it will take him three days to assemble the net. How will he support himself during the time he spends working on it? Before embarking on the project he will have to catch more fish than usual, so he will have some left over to sustain him during the several days he plans to devote to the net. Put another way, a pool of savings, which in this case takes the form of extra fish, has to exist in order for any production process, including this very simple one, to be completed.[18]

Crusoe is just one individual, but the principle he illustrates here applies to countries as well. Crusoe economics teaches us that if one individual engaged in an investment project, like Crusoe and his net, needs a pool of savings to see him through to its completion, then by extension an aggregate of capitalists spread over an entire economy likewise need a pool of savings to support them during *their* time-consuming production processes. Otherwise, they cannot complete their projects as planned.

Only real resources can see them through these processes. Printing up green pieces of paper and distributing them does not add to the pool of savings that is necessary to support them.

To get even closer to the heart of the problem with artificial credit creation, imagine a barter economy. Suppose a baker bakes ten loaves of bread, of which he consumes two and saves the other eight.[19] He then gives the eight remaining loaves to a shoemaker in exchange for a pair of shoes to be delivered the following week. The loaves of bread support the shoemaker as he goes about his craft. This example drawn from barter helps us to see the true nature of a credit transaction: real resources (in this case, loaves of bread) are transferred in exchange for other real resources (shoes). The baker cannot lend more loaves of bread than he has baked and saved. The only way he can increase the available credit to the shoemaker is by increasing the supply of real resources—e.g., by baking more loaves of bread.

This, at root, is why it is nonsensical to demand that the Fed inject "credit" into the economy. The Fed has no real resources to inject into the economy. Credit has to derive from real saved resources. Nothing can be lent that someone has not first saved.

The scenario does not fundamentally change when money is introduced. In a money economy, the baker sells his bread for dollars, and then lends the dollars to the shoemaker. The dollars represent claims to real resources. Flooding the economy with additional dollar bills that do not reflect claims to real resources does not and cannot increase the supply of real resources. All it can do is make the prices of existing resources go up as an increased supply of dollars chases an unchanged supply of goods.

Let's go back to our original baker/shoemaker example, except this time let's imagine one baker and *two* shoemakers. Let's suppose that the second shoemaker, like the first, needs to borrow eight loaves of bread to sustain him through his production process, and produces a pair of shoes in a week's time. The only way both shoemakers can be supported, therefore, is if the baker bakes and saves more loaves. He would need to save at least *sixteen* loaves—eight for each shoemaker—in order to advance them the credit necessary to support themselves during their production processes.

Now, in this money economy, let's imagine two scenarios.

Scenario 1. The baker bakes eighteen loaves of bread. He consumes two of the loaves himself, and sells the remaining loaves to a retail store at $1 each, for a total of $16. He saves this $16 in the bank. The bank, in turn, lends $8 to each shoemaker.

This economy is on a sustainable path. Enough real saving has taken place that all production projects can be completed.

Scenario 2. The baker bakes ten loaves of bread. He consumes two of the loaves himself, and sells the remaining loaves to a retail store at $1 each, for a total of $8. He saves this $8 in the bank. The bank, in turn, lends this $8 to one of the shoemakers. When the other shoemaker applies to borrow the $8 *he* needs, the bank just creates eight new dollars out of thin air and lends it to him.

This economy is not on a sustainable path. Not enough real saving has taken place for all production projects to be completed. Sure, each shoemaker has $8. But when they go to buy bread with this money, they will find that its price has risen. They will thereby discover that the money they have borrowed does not command enough real goods to sustain them.

This is what sensible economists mean when they say credit has to be based on real savings and cannot be created out of thin air. You can print up all the dollars you want, the Fed can give the banks as much money created out of thin air as it likes, but there is no avoiding the simple fact that there are only eight loaves of bread in existence. Ben Bernanke doesn't have any loaves of bread, and none of the financial tools at his disposal can produce any, either. All the monetary manipulation in the world cannot defy the constraints mercilessly imposed by reality.

The printing of the additional money is accompanied by no overall increase in the supply of bread, so when the shoemaker uses these new dollars to purchase bread, he necessarily draws resources away from other activities. The process of wealth generation is weakened when genuine wealth generators find themselves having to compete over resources with entrepreneurs who are engaged in bubble activities that can survive only as long as the credit spree continues.

Our example involving bakers and shoemakers involves an extremely simple and primitive economy, in which the unsustainability of the production processes involved becomes clear almost instantly. In a modern economy such as that of the United States, on the other hand, which is much more capital intensive, and in which the production process takes place in a series of stages, it takes longer for misallocations to reveal themselves. The two shoemakers learn quickly enough that their economy cannot support them both in their chosen field, and that one of them has misallocated his labor services. These problems take longer to be uncovered in a more advanced economy. But the principle is the same: since artificially created credit adds no additional resources to the economy, it puts the economy on a path that its pool of real savings cannot sustain.[20]

Anti-gold fallacies

The vast majority of those who condemn commodity money, and we may include economists here, have never read a thing on the subject, relying instead on a series of endlessly repeated fallacies that break down under the mildest scrutiny. On those rare occasions when they are forced to address the subject, some commentators actually reply that the idea of a commodity standard is old and passé, as if that is supposed to be an argument. These are a few of the traditional objections.

Gold and silver aren't flexible enough. We need money that is more flexible.

By "flexible," the critic actually means easily inflated by the government. Since that doesn't sound quite so innocent, "flexible" is used instead. In that sense, gold and silver are indeed inflexible. They cannot be created out of thin air to support constituencies that happen to be in favor. They cannot be endlessly duplicated, thereby wiping out the value of people's savings. That is not a disadvantage of gold and silver. It is a virtue.

The complaint that gold and silver are insufficiently "flexible" boils down to the crude argument that under a commodity standard there will be less lending to business, and therefore less economic growth. Since, under a commodity standard, bank notes can be redeemed into gold at any time, banks are less eager to print up additional, unbacked notes (or checking deposits) for lending to private firms, out of fear of a bank run. Banks need to be able to be more "flexible" so they can create money out of thin air and lend it. Then we'll become rich.

We have already seen the fallacy here. It's the failure once again to understand that money is not wealth. It's the failure to understand that the amount of lending that can take place is limited by the pool of real savings, not by how many unbacked pieces of paper can be printed up. A bank issuing loans based on credit it creates out of thin air, and which possesses no gold backing, is "flexible" enough to *make more loans*, but unless it has the magical ability to create real resources out of thin air, it can never increase the *number of projects* the economy can complete. Extra pieces of paper in people's hands simply allow them to compete with other people over an unchanged supply of goods, and thus can only shuffle those goods around the economy. Extra pieces of paper are not wealth and do not create wealth.

In short, printing up pieces of paper and lending them out is not a shortcut to wealth, which comes from saving, investment, hard work, and entrepreneurial skill.

Precious metals are too bulky.

Relatively little transport of precious metals from one bank to another needs to occur under a system of monetary freedom. It is in the banks' own interest to establish a clearing system whereby only the *net* changes in gold reserves between them need be physically transported from one institution to another. As for individuals carrying around coins, there is nothing to prevent debit cards from being used with a precious-metal money, and several institutions have already arisen to make that possible even now.

A gold standard is too costly; paper money is less expensive to produce.

The late Milton Friedman made this argument, though he had abandoned it by the end of his life. It is still heard from time to time.

This objection falls short for two reasons. One is that it thinks of "cost" too narrowly. It does indeed cost more to mine gold than it does to print paper bills. But is that really the only cost involved? As theory warns us and history shows, a government with the limitless power to issue unbacked legal-tender paper notes carries great costs of its own. We have already seen some of the costs of fiat money inflation. Government uses the ability to create money at will to enrich itself and its favored constituencies. When it creates the new money via credit markets it sets in motion the boom-bust cycle and all its associated wealth destruction. And so on.

When these costs are added to the ledger, the paper money system appears rather more expensive indeed.[21]

But even leaving out the costs society incurs from all the destructive consequences of paper money, it is not obvious that a gold standard would be more costly in terms of real resources than the system of fiat money coordinated by central banks that we have now. The German Bundesbank employed 11,400 people in 2007, the Banque de France 11,800 and the Federal Reserve System in the U.S. some 23,000, to name just three.[22] Those people all collect salaries, and have all been drawn away from employment in the production of useful goods and services.

Finally, the very fact that it *is* costly to mine gold and silver is one of the reasons these metals are particularly suitable for use as money. It is precisely because fiat paper money is practically costless that it is so dangerous. Governments can create any amount of it they want, and destroy the people's wealth in the process.

There isn't enough gold or silver to facilitate all the transactions of a modern economy.

Yes, there is. Since any supply of money is optimal above a certain threshold, the existing supply of gold or silver, combined with whatever additional quantities might be mined in the future, can indeed facilitate all transactions.* It is an old fallacy that says a given money supply can support only a limited number of transactions. David Ricardo answered it nearly two hundred years ago:

> If the quantity of gold or silver in the world employed as money
> were exceedingly small, or abundantly great . . . the variation in

---

*Most of the time a gold standard is actually a silver standard, with gold used for large transactions and silver for smaller ones. The important thing is that the government not attempt to establish a fixed ratio between the two metals, since it will inevitably overvalue one and undervalue the other, driving one out of circulation and disrupting the monetary system that people in the absence of governmental coercion would have freely adopted.

their quantity would have produced no other effect than to make the commodities for which they were exchanged comparatively dear or cheap. The smaller quantity of money would perform the functions of a circulating medium as well as the larger.[23]

Remember that what really happens in an economy that uses money is that *goods exchange against other goods*, and the exchanges are simply *denominated* in money—gold, silver, whatever. The precious metal is just the intermediary. If there is relatively little of the precious metal to go around, prices will be high. So will wages and incomes. Here we see money's role as a *numéraire* that establishes exchange rates between all goods in the economy. A *numéraire* function can be carried out by any supply of a precious metal. (Within reason, of course—in the extremely unlikely event that there were suddenly only seven atoms of silver left on earth, the rest having been whisked away by aliens, the market would shift into copper or some other money.)

This, in fact, is how the American standard of living increased in the nineteenth century: a relatively constant money supply combined with an ever-increasing supply of other goods yielded lower prices, so people could acquire more of the things they wanted for less money.

The supply of gold cannot keep up with the growth in business activity.

This is just a variant of the previous objection. Why should it need to, and why would that be desirable? As we have seen, the same supply of money can accommodate any amount of commerce. As output increases, the monetary unit simply gains in purchasing power. It is to misconceive the nature and purpose of money completely to think its supply needs to expand in order to allow more transactions to take place. It is not the end of the world if prices fall over time and the value of money rises. That was the case throughout much of American history, in fact. Trying to increase the money supply in order to offset this fall in prices or to keep the money supply growing along with business activity would simply sow the seeds of the business cycle, as we have seen.[24]

Simply put, the main criticisms against gold are either short-sighted or fallacious. Henry Hazlitt, who in saner times wrote editorials on economic topics for the *New York Times*, stated the whole matter very simply: "The tremendous merit of gold is, if we want to put it that way, a negative one: it is *not* a managed paper money that can ruin everyone who is legally forced to accept it or who puts his confidence in it. *The technical criticisms of the gold standard become utterly trivial when compared with this single merit.*"[25]

Hazlitt is right. So many fallacies and so much superstition have grown up around these important topics, though, that rational discussion about them has become almost impossible.

Entire books have been written just on the disadvantages and dangers of fiat money, and the strengths and virtues of a commodity money freely adopted by the market; here we can be content to chip away at the propaganda against sound money and get Americans thinking in new and promising ways. You do not win friends in the political and media establishments by proposing a monetary system that cannot be exploited by governments to enrich their friends, enable their addiction to spending and looting, and fund their bailouts. But when you ask a question that sends respectable opinion into hysterics, that's often a sign you're on the right track.

A Note on Deflation

The mainstream media, including even the business press, has been full of irrational and hysterical warnings about deflation. Like *inflation, deflation* saw its definition change over the course of the twentieth century. Once defined as a decrease in the money supply, it now refers in common parlance to a decline in consumer prices. Whether it refers to an actual decline in the supply of money or just a fall in consumer prices, deflation is considered the great menace of our time. Not surprisingly, then, one of the arguments against a commodity money is that it either leads to, or cannot prevent, deflation.

Critics who level this charge do not generally mean that the supply of gold actually decreases over time, since in fact the supply of gold slowly increases. The argument is that the growth in the supply of gold does not keep up with the growth in the supply of all other goods, and that the result is falling prices. Falling prices supposedly cause economic hard times.

But of course falling prices do not cause economic hard times. They are the natural outcome of a progressing market economy. Under a commodity money, there is a natural tendency for consumer prices to fall over time. The money supply stays relatively constant or increases at a modest rate, but the increasing capital investment and resulting productivity gains of a market economy typically generate yearly increases in the production of goods and services. Simply put, since we have more stuff and about the same amount of money, the price of goods will fall. There is nothing sinister or economically problematic about this healthy process, which economist Joseph Salerno calls "growth deflation." It characterized the American economy from 1789 through 1913, a period in which the American economy reached extraordinary heights of prosperity. China has lived through a growth deflation in recent years: from 1998 to 2001, general retail prices declined in each of those years anywhere from 0.8 to 3.0 percent, at the same time that real GDP increased at an annual average rate of 7.6 percent.*

We have grown accustomed, living under a fiat currency, to seeing prices rise more or less steadily year after year. Most of us just assume *that's just what happens*—prices go up over time. But even in the inflationary environment created by our fiat currency, we can point to sector-specific growth deflation: in high-tech products. Computer prices have declined dramatically, and yet computer firms continue to prosper. In 1999, after all this "deflation," computer firms were shipping some 43 million units, as compared to only 490,000 in 1980, despite a 90 percent decrease in their products' quality-adjusted prices. Consumers have obviously benefited.

An economy-wide growth deflation would benefit consumers all the more. This, in fact, is how living standards are raised: more capital investment makes the economy more physically productive, and the increased supply of goods leads to lower prices. Falling prices: this is the unspeakable terror that the Fed promises to save us from, no matter how much money it has to create out of thin air to do so. Peter Schiff rightly complains that "under the guise of 'price stability,' generally defined as annual price rises of 2–3 percent, the government robs its citizens of all the benefits of falling prices and uses the loot to buy votes, thereby trading the rising living standards of their constituents for their own reelection."**

---

*Joseph T. Salerno, "An Austrian Taxonomy of Deflation—With Applications to the U.S.," *Quarterly Journal of Austrian Economics* 6 (Winter 2003): 84.

**Peter D. Schiff, *Crash Proof: How to Profit from the Coming Economic Collapse* (New York: Wiley, 2006), 80.

So much for price deflation; what if the money supply itself decreases? When banks fail, for instance, all the money they created out of thin air disappears along with them. Under a commodity money, it is true that the government would not have the tools to try to push prices back up (as it inevitably and stupidly tries to do) in the wake of a decrease in the money supply. That is a good thing. When the market is trying to re-establish the rational pricing of goods in terms of supply and demand in the wake of a previous inflation of the money supply, the government's further manipulation of the money supply can only create distortions and hamper this healthy process.

More to the point, under a commodity money, we would never have had the inflated prices in the first place, since the money supply wouldn't substantially increase: the banking system finds it very difficult to create paper money out of thin air without provoking massive redemption claims of paper into the commodity.

Poor economic performance doesn't result from falling prices. Falling prices sometimes result from the popping of an inflationary bubble. When prices decline in the wake of a previous bout of inflation, capital and labor are being reallocated into sustainable production processes, and no increases in consumer welfare can be brought about by interfering in this purgative process.*

It is the role of the entrepreneur to anticipate *all* the variables affecting the market for his product—not just input costs and consumer prices, but also the supply of money, the relative health of the banking system and the stock market, and the like. If he expects prices to fall or even the supply of money to decrease (because inflationary banks may be on the verge of closing their doors), he responds by lowering the prices he's willing to pay for labor, parts,

---

*Mark Thornton, "Apoplithorismosphobia," *Quarterly Journal of Austrian Economics* 6 (Winter 2003): 8.

wholesale goods—what economists call the "factors of production."* One may object: what if the firms that produce these factors of production refuse to accept the lower bids for their goods? If they do, that necessarily means they are getting better offers and are able to sell at higher prices elsewhere. Profitability does therefore exist elsewhere in the economy. If our entrepreneur cannot purchase the factors of production he needs at prices that would make his enterprise profitable, he is in exactly the same situation as any entrepreneur who finds that people aren't willing to pay him enough for what he's selling.**

Of course, the best way to avoid a bank-credit deflation and any calculation problems it might cause is not to inflate the money supply artificially in the first place—yet another benefit of a commodity money whose supply government cannot manipulate.

In 2004 the Papers and Proceedings of the *American Economic Review* included an empirical study of deflationary episodes in seventeen countries over the past one hundred years.*** When the authors excluded the Great Depression, they found that, in 90 percent of the deflation episodes they studied, no depression resulted.

---

*Thanks to Jörg Guido Hüslmann for this point.

**Consider the hardest case, one involving a systemic economic depression accompanied by deflation. Deflation-phobes argue that businesses must fail in that environment, since the prices of their inputs remain the same while the prices of their products and the revenue they earn from them go down. But this is an error. If their revenues go down, then they have less money with which to purchase factors of production (i.e., inputs). That decreased demand for the factors of production in turn lowers the prices of the factors, and the alleged problem is solved.

***Andrew Atkeson and Patrick J. Kehoe, "Deflation and Depression: Is There an Empirical Link?" *American Economic Review* Papers and Proceedings 94 (May 2004): 99–103. See also Joseph T. Salerno, "Deflation and Depression: Where's the Link?" Mises.org, August 6, 2004, http://mises.org/story/1583.

"In a broader historical context, beyond the Great Depression, the notion that deflation and depression are linked virtually disappears," they concluded.* Falling prices in and of themselves are not a cause of business depression—they've occurred far too often during prosperous times for that to be true—and are more likely a consequence of depressed economic conditions rather than a cause of them.

---

*The standard claim that the Great Depression was caused by deflation, a view advanced with particular vigor by Milton Friedman and Anna Schwartz, is based on the previously accepted empirical claim that deflation episodes are associated with depressions. But since the most recent research finds no such link between deflation and depression, the Friedman-Schwartz account of the Great Depression no longer persuades, if it ever did. Much better accounts of the Depression can be found in Murray N. Rothbard, *America's Great Depression*, 4th ed. (New York: Richardson & Snyder, 1983) and Lionel Robbins, *The Great Depression* (London: Macmillan, 1934).

CHAPTER 7

WHAT NOW?

The United States need not be bogged down in recession for years and years. The free market may yet transition us out of the current mess swiftly and efficiently, though not without some unavoidable pain, as it did during the much more severe downturn of 1920–21. The market is trying to adjust asset prices downward, toward where they belong, in order for growth to occur once again. It is also attempting, quite properly, to ration credit at a time of uncertainty, and to slow the growth of indebtedness. Many bad loans have been made, and as those disappear from the books (either through foreclosure or some other legal settlement) banks are sometimes choosing not to replace them one-for-one with new loans, and in fact there is no particular reason they should. These are all good things. Even the market for credit default swaps, the financial instrument that has fueled so much of the attack on the free market, is actually doing better than the (regulated) bond market as of this writing, and was relatively stable amid the economic and political turmoil of 2008.

But any readjustment to normal economic conditions, and the restoration of prosperity, can be stalled or prevented by sufficiently foolish government activity. And there is no shortage of bad suggestions on that front. Bailouts of all kinds of companies and institutions are being contemplated, which divert capital from healthy institutions to unhealthy ones and deprive the latter of the new leadership that bankruptcy would bring. Barack Obama's tax policy involves raising taxes on wealthier Americans (he is apparently not satisfied with the 68 percent of all income taxes that that the top 10 percent of earners already pay) while lowering them for the less wealthy. The net effect of that tax policy will almost certainly be to encourage spending at the expense of saving, and surely that's the point—the superstition that stimulating consumption is good for a depressed economy is alive and well. That same superstition lies behind the hundreds of billions of dollars—perhaps a trillion—proposed in new "stimulus" spending by the government. We borrowed and spent our way into this crisis, and our political class expects to borrow and spend its way out.

"Spend if you love America"

Let's begin by dismissing politicians' favorite strategy for getting us out of our slump: make the people spend.[1] Behind every government "stimulus" effort—whether it's Barack Obama's massive infrastructure programs or George W. Bush's checks to every American, is the belief that consumer spending drives the economy.

There is a kernel of truth in this otherwise illogical view. Consumer spending does drive the economy in the sense that every firm decides on what it will produce, with what methods, and in what quantities, in light of what it anticipates consumer demand to be. Businesses don't survive unless they create what the consuming public wants. So consumers drive the economy in the sense that their wishes are what motivate the production decisions of producers.

But "consumer spending drives the economy" is often taken to mean that wealth is generated by the mere fact of our spending—and this belief is provably false.

Whenever a recession threatens to hit, Americans are urged to rush out and empty their wallets to get the economy back on track. But what is supposed to happen next, when the following day Americans have no more money to spend? That's left unexplained. Saving is especially condemned, even though it's obviously the prudent and sensible thing to do during a recession. A penny saved, we're told, is a penny diverted from immediate spending—it's actually said to be a drag on the economy. It was this fallacy on which the "stimulus package" of 2008 (and so many other foolish programs like it) was based.

The spending-is-good-for-the-economy fallacy grows partly out of our use of Gross Domestic Product as a measure of economic health. GDP sums up the dollar value of all final goods and services sold in a country in a given year. It thereby leaves out all the higher and intermediate stages of production that take place on the way to producing final consumer goods, since these processes are the *ingredients* of final goods, but not final goods in themselves. But this higher-stage production is the bulk of the economy, and leaving it out gives a distorted picture of the percentage of the overall economy that consumer spending amounts to.[2]

Even without examining the statistics on which this idea is based—its proponents claim that consumption spending is over 70 percent of the economy—it should be obvious that something isn't quite right about it. Consumption is the act of *using things up*. How did any country ever become rich simply by using things up? Before things can be used up, they need to be *produced*. Production, in fact, is what makes consumption possible in the first place, because it gives us the means with which we can acquire the goods we want. To consume more, we first have to produce something ourselves.

Where does a consumer shopping at a retail store get the purchasing power that allows him to make his purchase and consume in the first place? He gets the money he spends from contributing to some previous *production process*. He earns a paycheck by playing a role in *producing* something people want.

John Stuart Mill already refuted the fallacy that consumer spending drove the economy nearly two centuries ago. "What a country wants to make it richer is never consumption, but production," he wrote. "Where there is the latter, we may be sure that there is no want [lack] of the former. To produce, implies that the producer desires to consume; why else should he give himself useless labor? He may not wish to consume what he himself produces, but his motive for producing and selling is the desire to buy. Therefore, if the producers generally produce and sell more and more, they certainly also buy more and more."[3]

And as Austrian business cycle theory shows, the last thing we should want to do during an economic downturn is to give an artificial stimulus to consumption. The downturn itself is caused by an increase in consumption simultaneously with an (incompatible) increase in investment. Stimulating more consumption will only widen the mismatch between resources invested in higher-order stages of production geared toward future production on the one hand and demand for consumer goods in the immediate present on the other. That's why economist Gottfried von Haberler, speaking during the Great Depression, warned about "a one-sided strengthening of the purchasing power of the consumer, because it was precisely this disproportional increase of demand for consumers' goods which precipitated the crisis."[4]

The usual fallacy that comes in reply is that if we increase our productive capacity too much, we'll have general overproduction: the economy will produce more goods than people can afford. This Leninist critique of markets and their alleged tendency toward overproduction has been thoughtlessly accepted by the media, and indeed by just about everyone. But it, too, is an absurdity: the increased production is precisely what gives people the wherewithal to buy the newly created goods. And the more goods we produce, the less expensive in terms of money they will be, thereby making it possible for people to buy the increased supply. As we noted above, a consumer is able to buy things only because he himself has produced things in the past. Thus it is production that makes consumption possible. As long as firms produce things consumers want in the proportions they want, therefore, the more we produce the more we can consume.[5] The contention that there can never be a general over-production of all goods, and that increased supplies of goods themselves constitute the demand for other goods, is known as Say's Law, after economist J. B. Say. (John Maynard Keynes famously claimed to have refuted Say's Law but, as usual with Keynes, he did so only by misstating the law and then refuting his own misstatement.[6])

Think of all the houses that were built during the recent American housing bubble. Government policy, including the cheap credit policy of the Federal Reserve, encouraged this excess of home building. The boom in home purchases in turn led many people to believe that house prices would continue ever upward. As a result, we might say there was an "overproduction" of homes. But there certainly was not a *general* over-production of all goods in the economy. All the resources—capital, labor, parts, land, etc.—poured into making houses would have gone elsewhere if not for this building boom. Entrepreneurial error or government interference can produce overproduction in a particular economic sector—but only to the extent that other sectors underproduce. The overproduced sector, in a market economy, will suffer as prices go down and costs of production go up, which then drives businesses out of that sector and frees up resources for other sectors.

The difference between production and consumption

Adam Smith made an important distinction between consumptive expenditure (or nonproductive consumption) and productive expenditure (or productive consumption). Consumptive expenditure uses up some good without providing for its replacement, such as when a person wears out an air conditioner in his home after a series of hot summers. Productive expenditure involves using something up in order to create still more (and/or more valuable) resources in the future. Investing in machinery that increases productivity is an example of productive expenditure, since a machine can often produce far more goods than were expended in building the machine itself. Consumptive expenditure uses up, exhausts, and destroys; productive expenditure provides for its own replacement in the form of an increased supply of goods in the future. Smith put it this way:

> A thousand ploughmen consume fully as much corn and cloth in the course of a year as a regiment of soldiers. But the difference between the kinds of consumption is immense. The labor of the ploughman has, during the year, served to call into existence a quantity of property, which not only repays the corn and cloth which he has consumed, but repays it with a profit. The soldier on the other hand produces nothing. What he has consumed is gone, and its place is left absolutely vacant. The country is the poorer for his consumption, to the full amount of what he has consumed. It is not the poorer, but the richer for what the ploughman has consumed, because, during the time he was consuming it, he has reproduced what does more than replace it.[7]

In effect, then, when we're being urged to consume more in order to "help the economy," or when the government engages in "stimulus" packages meant to encourage consumer spending, they are suggesting we'd all be better off if we used up a lot of things without providing the resources for their replacement. Just take and take and take—and that will make everyone rich!

And incidentally, money that people save is not a drain on the economy. Just the opposite. Savings provide the pool from which business can draw to build new, more productive equipment that can produce capital and consumer goods in ever-greater quantities at lower costs in the future. Without saving, without abstention from consumption, this process, and the increase in living standards that accompanies it, could not occur.

We are much wealthier now than we were 300 years ago not because we consume more today. We consume more today because we can produce much more, and it is this production that itself both fuels our ability to consume and increases our standard of living.

"Stimulus" packages that encourage both private nonproductive consumption and public nonproductive consumption (i.e., federal spending) will only intensify the present crisis and hollow out the economy's productive capacity still further. And on top of that, they seek to strengthen the economy by the obviously paradoxical means of building roads and bridges funded by more debt—like a homeowner who decides to solve his debt problem by borrowing more money to remodel his house.[8] *It makes no sense*, so it's no surprise that our leaders favor it.

What to do

To restore the economy to health in the short run, and to build a foundation for genuine prosperity rather than the phony, capital-consuming kind that comes from artificial credit expansion or Keynesian "stimulus," a number of important free-market reforms should be made.

Let them go bankrupt.

First, the idea of bankruptcy should not be so unthinkable as the Fed and the Treasury consider it. A firm doesn't disappear when it declares bankruptcy. Its capital equipment and its assets continue to exist. But they pass out of the hands of those who have failed to employ them in ways that best satisfy the public, and into the hands of those more likely to do a capable job. If they in turn should fail, these assets will pass into the possession of still other owners. Enron was the largest energy company in the United States. Its bankruptcy in 2001 had no effect on the economy at all, and even energy markets barely noticed it.

Economist Steven Landsburg asks "what's special about banks" that makes them deserve a bailout that would never be granted to firms in most other industries. The usual answer is that lending would come to a halt, business would not be able to raise needed funds, and so on. But banks are merely intermediaries between depositors and borrowers. Presumably this intermediation could occur in another form. In our day and age it is far easier for would-be lenders and borrowers to find each other outside the banking system. If a firm wants to raise capital, couldn't it sell bonds over the Internet, issue stock, or borrow overseas? "I'm not sure these big Wall Street banks are really necessary, and I'm not sure we'd miss them much if they were gone," Landsburg says.[9]

Abolish Fannie and Freddie.

Next, the U.S. government should stop exposing itself to the vagaries of the real estate market. The executive branch first seized Fannie and Freddie, and Congress then increased the amount of money they could spend on mortgages. These zombie companies have already drawn enough of the mortgage market away from where truly free-market channels, unencumbered by firms with state-granted monopoly privileges like Fannie and Freddie, would have taken it. "The fact that government bears such a huge responsibility for the current mess," argues Harvard's Jeffrey Miron, "means any response should eliminate the conditions that created this situation in the first place, not attempt to fix bad government with more government." That means, at a minimum, "getting rid of Fannie Mae and Freddie Mac."[10] Miron is right: Fannie and Freddie should be put into bankruptcy receivership, and their assets auctioned off to private mortgage guarantors. Certainly its mortgage-reduction program, with all its unfairness and moral hazard, should be discontinued immediately.

People who disbelieved Barack Obama's rhetoric about "change" were sternly lectured for their supposedly undue cynicism. But early indications are that the cynics were right: "change" means more bailouts and a less free market—the very same economic program of the presidential administration Obama so sharply criticized—and government personnel drawn from the same revolving-door pool of New York and Washington insiders who were blindsided by the crisis, including (as chief of staff) a former director of Freddie Mac. If Obama wants to prove he is serious about change and that his presidential tenure will be truly historic, he will pledge that under his watch there will be no bailouts of any private company for any reason. A few high-profile bankruptcies should send a consistent enough message. Right now the principle appears to be that small-scale losses, the kind racked up by small business, must be borne by the parties involved, but inefficiency and mismanagement on a stupendous scale can win their perpetrators special benefits. (Although, as we saw with Lehman, even this principle is not consistently observed, such that a cloud of uncertainty continues to hang over the economy.) To say the least, rewarding losers puts the wrong incentives in place. The message from the public should be clear: large-scale failures are too big to be allowed to burden other, more efficient producers. They are not too big to fail.

Stop the bailouts and cut government spending.

Government spending, as well as all other forms of government predation on the economy, must be scaled back swiftly and radically. Government activity itself siphons off resources from real wealth generators. As usual, the U.S. government should do exactly the opposite of what the *New York Times* calls for. That means a drastic reduction in government spending, in order to free up resources for wealth-generating activity. That means no more new trillion-dollar entitlement promises, and no more trillion-dollar foreign policy.[11] It certainly means Paul Krugman should be studiously ignored when he says the Obama administration should come up with a figure it thinks necessary to stimulate the economy and then increase it by 50 percent.

Problems caused by excessive spending and indebtedness cannot be cured by more spending and more indebtedness, any more than the cure for excessive lending is more excessive lending. During the Great Depression, FDR's Treasury secretary, Henry Morgenthau, noted in his diary: "We have tried spending money. We are spending more than we have ever spent before and it does not work.... We have never made good on our promises.... I say after eight years of this Administration we have just as much unemployment as when we started...and an enormous debt to boot!"[12]

It is not simply that government spending has reduced the pool of savings and relatively impoverished the population, though that is of course true. But when government runs deficits (that is, when it spends more than it receives in taxes) and borrows the money to make up the difference, it pushes interest rates upward. If the Fed is coordinating its injections of new money with reference to a particular interest rate—if it has an interest rate target, in other words—then the higher interest rates caused by deficit spending mean the Fed has to inject ever more money to force rates back down to the target again. In that way, government borrowing encourages further money creation and thus the continuing debasement of the dollar.

End government manipulation of money.

Money itself may be the most socialized sector in the American economy. The present system of fiat paper money was established by the seizure of private property, when Americans were required to relinquish all their monetary gold in 1933. The dollar is inflated by a central bank, established by an act of Congress and whose board is appointed by the president, that enjoys monopoly privileges and can manipulate the money supply as it likes. Legal-tender laws force people to accept a money that may be declining in value, and thus makes the introduction of alternatives very difficult.

What exactly is "laissez faire" about any of this? And yet we are told incessantly that laissez faire has failed. In fact, it is central planning of the money supply and interest rates that has failed. It has given us the most bloated asset bubble the world has ever seen. It has encouraged the diversion of resources into an unsustainable structure of production that must be rearranged amidst inevitable bankruptcies and liquidations.

And no, this is not better than what we had before. Money and banking have never been entirely free in American history, which is the history of government-established national banks, special privileges for unsound banks, disruptive government-imposed gold-silver ratios, and the like. The gold standard had already been seriously debased by the time of the 1920s (though that hasn't stopped historians from trying to blame the Great Depression, foolishly enough, on gold). But when Americans had a legitimate commodity standard, they had a money that held its value. In fact, it actually gained in value. An item that cost $100 in 1820 would have cost only $63.02 in 1913.[13]

Put the Fed on the table.

It is also long past time that the Federal Reserve be put back on the table as a subject for debate. The Fed postures as the great rock of stability in the American economy, but it is responsible for more economic *instability* than any other institution. It is an unnecessary and disruptive intrusion into the marketplace. And because as far as American politics is concerned the Fed may as well not exist—and thus the Fed's policies are essentially never a subject for debate in the American public square— the chaos it creates is inevitably blamed on "capitalism" and made the pretext for additional rounds of government intervention.

Investment adviser Jim Rogers predicts the Fed will be abolished within the next ten years. That may be too optimistic, but the very fact that the possibility is raised by a figure like Rogers, whose predictions about and assessments of the economy have been consistently correct, indicates that we may at last be turning an intellectual corner. And not a moment too soon.

The Fed is responsible for elevating moral hazard into a permanent feature of banking. Banks can not only safely lend beyond their reserves, but they can also make credit available to more risky ventures, in the knowledge that the Fed's discount window and "lender of last resort" authority are available to them if anything should go terribly wrong. Thanks to deposit "insurance," bank runs are also much less likely than they would otherwise be. And if the Fed or FDIC do not bail them out, there is always the Treasury and the U.S. taxpayer. What bank manager, looking at a higher salary and bigger stock options, *wouldn't* take on additional risk in an environment like that? The gamble certainly seems worth the artificially diminished risk.

By the end of 2008, the Fed had lent trillions of dollars to various private parties, as part of both the official bailout package and of some additional lending programs beyond that. It refused to identify the recipients of many of these loans or what it was accepting as collateral. If the Fed is accepting risky collateral—and it has been consistently liberalizing its collateral requirements—then it is putting taxpayers on the hook for substantial losses and without even disclosing their nature or the parties involved.

Bloomberg News (which as of this writing is taking the Fed to court for the release of this information), the financial news network, reported: "Fed chairman Ben S. Bernanke and Treasury Secretary Henry Paulson said in September they would comply with congressional demands for transparency in a $700 billion bailout of the banking system. Two months later, as the Fed lends far more than that in separate rescue programs that didn't require approval by Congress, Americans have no idea where their money is going or what securities the banks are pledging in return."[14] At what point do Americans, and supporters of the free market in particular, finally decide that the situation is out of control and the time has come for some new ideas?

Close those special lending windows.

In the short run, the Fed should abolish its Term Auction Facilities and return to making loans at its discount window only to its traditional customers. Interest rates should be allowed to float, so they can perform their crucial coordinating function at a time of such fragility in the market. The Greenspan and Bernanke puts should be abandoned, as should any further "bailout" efforts. The Fed has done quite enough to the economy already. The market deserves a chance.

End the monopoly money.

Central planning, monopoly privilege, and the suppression of competition, all of which characterize the Federal Reserve and the American banking system, are the very opposite of the free market. Even a writer for the *Wall Street Journal*, which has not been sympathetic to the classical gold standard, noted how at odds with the basic principles of the free market the Federal Reserve is. At the end of September 2008, Judy Shelton wrote: "If capitalism depends on designating a person of godlike abilities to manage demand and supply for all forms of money and credit—currency, demand deposits, money-market funds, repurchase agreements, equities, mortgages, corporate debt—we are as doomed as those wretched citizens who relied on central planning for their economic salvation." Capital, the array of goods that contribute to the production process, is rather an important ingredient of capitalism. And yet alleged believers in the free market somehow manage to bring themselves to "allow the price of capital, i.e., the interest rate on loanable funds, to be fixed by a central committee in accordance with government objectives. We might as well resurrect Gosplan, the old Soviet State Planning Committee, and ask them to draw up the next five-year plan."[15]

In 1949 a frustrated Allan Sproul, who was then the president of the New York Fed, declared before the American Bankers Association: "The principal argument for restoring the circulation of gold coin seems to be distrust of the money managers and of the fiscal policies of government."[16] Sproul deserves credit for understanding what is at stake: we don't trust the government, and that's why we want to do away with its discretion over money. This point would be obvious to most people were it not for all the economic superstitions that have been spread about the wickedness of commodity money and the wondrous benefits of a paper money issued by our wise rulers.

Some people have sensibly called for a return to the gold standard, or some kind of commodity standard, to replace the failed system of fiat money. Others, though, have suggested that the time may have come to go beyond even this. The very word "standard," these critics argue, is unhelpful. It is not a "gold standard" or a "silver standard" as such that we should seek. It is not a *standard* at all. "Standards" can be manipulated by government and are imposed monopolistically. The "gold standard" of the nineteenth century as it existed in the West, for instance, often involved the coercive suppression of alternative monies. Instead, they say, what we should favor is the simple idea of freedom, that people are capable of choosing the medium of exchange that suits them best and that most reliably performs the functions of money.[17] As we have seen, money originates out of the voluntary choices of individuals seeking to facilitate their transactions within the division of labor. It does not depend on government. We can even say that there is no role government can play in the monetary system that can confer any kind of social benefit.

As Ludwig von Mises once said, the history of money is the history of government efforts to destroy money. If ever there was a monopoly with which government could not be trusted, this is it. The temptation to debase the money and impoverish the people in order to benefit favored constituencies, hoping most people won't know the source of their declining standard of living, is too great. The present monetary system encourages risk and recklessness, with financial firms accumulating ever-higher pyramids of debt on top of a small sliver of equity—just the opposite of the much higher equity ratios banks maintained even in the imperfect nineteenth century. And as we have seen, the central bank's inflation of the money supply by its increases in bank reserves is responsible for the boom-bust cycle. During the bust phase, firms that made unsound investments, if they are large enough, then demand that the government's money monopoly now be used to bail them out. They tend to get what they want.

Is this so obviously the best conceivable system that any non-trivial alternatives are to be dismissed out of hand?

Over three decades ago, free-market economist and Nobel Laureate F. A. Hayek called for nothing less than the separation of money and state. "I am more convinced than ever," he said, "that if we ever again are going to have a decent money, it will not come from government: it will be issued by private enterprise, because providing the public with good money which it can trust and use can not only be an extremely profitable business; it imposes on the issuer a discipline to which the government has never been and cannot be subject. It is a business which competing enterprise can maintain only if it gives the public as good a money as anybody else." He continued:

There is no justification in history for the existing position of a government monopoly of issuing money. It has never been proposed on the ground that government will give us better money than anybody else could. It has always, since the privilege of issuing money was first explicitly represented as a Royal prerogative, been advocated because the power to issue money was essential for the finance of the government—not in order to give us good money, but in order to give to government access to the tap where it can draw the money it needs by manufacturing it. That, ladies and gentlemen, is not a method by which we can hope ever to get good money. To put it into the hands of an institution which is protected against competition, which can force us to accept the money, which is subject to incessant political pressure, such an authority will not ever again give us good money.[18]

There would be no need to abolish the *instruments* with which we are familiar, like credit and debit cards, checks, and paper money. There is only a need to change the rules that govern the institutions that issue them.[19] An important step forward involves the repeal of legal tender laws, which require acceptance of the dollar as a form of payment. These laws are a monopolistic intrusion into the free market. Right now they (along with sales and capital-gains taxes on gold and silver) stand in the way of the spontaneous introduction of other media of exchange that people expect to hold their value better than the politically manipulated U.S. dollar. If the law can force people to accept payments in the depreciated currency, voluntary efforts to introduce currency competition will come to naught. If the government's money has to be accepted, any other kind of money is put at an artificial disadvantage.

Various transition plans from our current fiat paper standard back to a commodity standard have been proposed by economists, and we refer to them in the notes, but the simple changes described here would go a long way toward freeing the market in money and thereby giving

Americans the utility-enhancing opportunity to choose between monies that lose value over time and can be manipulated against their will, and monies that gain value over time.[20]

Present disabilities notwithstanding, various private firms have already begun to establish services by which people can make transactions in gold, using financial instruments like debit cards with which we have become familiar. With the advent of the Internet and the growth in computer technology, conditions have never been easier or more auspicious for the use of precious metals as money.[21]

They told us so

The Austrian approach to understanding what has happened to the economy holds far greater explanatory power than does any competing school of thought. Learning about the Austrian point of view is especially urgent for those conservatives and libertarians who think of themselves as defenders of the free society and the free market. Some conservative writers and publications have made the mistake of blaming the financial crisis on the Community Reinvestment Act. That approach is a dead end. The CRA may have played a modest role in the collapse, but a debacle of this magnitude obviously requires a more substantial explanation. We are watching a systemic problem unfold, and looking for ways to blame it all on "the Democrats" is unhelpful. It is the monetary system itself, a system that enjoys wide bipartisan support, that is breaking down, and it is the federal government's intervention into *this* aspect of our lives, far more than its push for subprime mortgages, that threatens our economic well-being and accounts for what happened.

In short, supporters of the market economy need to decide once and for all whether they really believe their own arguments. People who argue for "fiscal responsibility" will never get anywhere, and cannot be taken seriously, as long as they tolerate a system in which the government can create out of thin air all the money it wants. If the federal government is an addict, then the Federal Reserve System is its enabler.

If you believe in the free market, you cannot support the Fed, one of the most intrusive interventions into the market. If you believe in the free market, you cannot support central planning of money, the very lifeblood of the economy. If you believe in the free market, you cannot support government price-fixing, including the fixing of interest rates. No free-market supporter worth his salt would accept the argument that thus-and-so is so important that it needs to be administered and supplied by government. In any other context, free-market advocates know the correct answer: the more important a sector is, the worse a job government would do with it, and the more urgently it needs to be handled by free individuals subject to competition. Money may in fact be far better cared for within the nexus of voluntary cooperation that constitutes the free market than under the compulsion and coercion of government.

Normally the supporter of the market economy looks to some government intervention to account for a disruption of the economy: price controls, tax increases, subsidies, and the like. While a handful of government programs and agencies helped direct our made-up money and credit to certain sectors, the hot air that filled the bubble was generated by the Fed. There are a few competing traditions of free-market economic thought, but only one, the Austrian School of Mises and Hayek, emphasizes the role of the Fed in disrupting the market economy.

In short, those who correctly support the free market no longer have a choice: they need to consider the Austrian School, which offers the only intellectually coherent free-market position in light of the present crisis. Conservatives and libertarians, and indeed all Americans, should acquaint themselves with the great works of some of the most scandalously neglected minds of the twentieth century, all of whom warned of the chickens that are now—unfortunately but inevitably—coming home to roost.

The Austrians, surely the fastest-growing school of economic thought in the world, have been neglected long enough. The economic mainstream, so called, told everyone in the 1920s that depressions were a thing of the past and in the 1990s that a new economy had arrived.[22] The vast majority of economists likewise failed to see the present crisis coming. In each case, the Austrians saw what everyone else missed. Doesn't that earn them a teensy weensy bit of credit, and make their tradition of economic science worth investigating?

The best way to avoid the bursting of economic bubbles and to clean up the wreckage caused by artificial booms is to not initiate artificial booms in the first place. We should at last abandon our superstitions about the expertise of Fed officials and their ability to manage our monetary system. It's about time we listened instead to people who have a coherent theory to explain why these crises occur, saw *this* crisis coming, and have something to suggest other than juvenile fantasies about spending and inflating our way to prosperity. The choice is a stark one: we can follow the very suggestions that prolonged the Great Depression and gave Japan its slump of nearly two decades, or we can try a different approach, one with an excellent track record and that is based on a theory that actually accounts for what is happening.

Now *that* would be change we can believe in.

ACKNOWLEDGMENTS

A time-sensitive book like this is necessarily the product of fast and in-tense work, and it would have been much more difficult without the help of friends and family. I am grateful for helpful conversations with economists Peter Klein of the University of Missouri, Roger Garrison of Auburn University, Mark Thornton of the Ludwig von Mises Institute, Jörg Guido Hülsmann of the University of Angers (France), Grove City College economics department chairman Jeffrey Herbener, and Joseph Salerno, professor of economics and graduate program chair at Pace University. Robert P. Murphy and Michael Rozeff also answered a few im-portant questions along the way. Special thanks to Mark Thornton for commenting on several chapters, and to Lew Rockwell both for reading the entire manuscript and for being such a generous benefactor to me over the years. Any errors of fact or interpretation are solely my own.

If we valued truth, these and other important scholars would be looked to as the experts who can lead us back to prosperity. But

Mencken may have been on to something: "The truth, indeed, is something that mankind, for some mysterious reason, instinctively dislikes. Every man who tries to tell it is unpopular, and even when, by the sheer strength of his case, he prevails, he is put down as a scoundrel."

I'm also grateful to the folks at Regnery Publishing for taking on this project, and specifically to Tim Carney, my editor, for helping make the finished product so much better than my initial draft. Thanks also to Congressman Ron Paul for his generous foreword, which he supplied to me in the middle of doing the 53 other things he somehow manages to juggle at once.

Thanks to my friends in the Auburn Area Community Theatre for giving me an enjoyable break from this project several nights a week during their fall production of *The Odd Couple*, in which I played Vinnie.

My mother, Walda Woods, provided babysitting services and other support at critical moments as the manuscript was at last coming together.

Finally, I cannot thank Heather, my wife, enough for her support of this project. She has tolerated a (somewhat recovering) workaholic husband for over six years now. I owe her a respite.

APPENDIX: FURTHER READING

A book of this length cannot, and is not intended to, answer all questions or objections. It is a starting point on the road to further reading and learning.

For the layman, I recommend a few relatively short books aimed at a nonspecialist audience. Essential among them are the works of Murray N. Rothbard, particularly *What Has Government Done to Our Money?* and *The Case Against the Fed*. A longer and more detailed treatment of the issues raised in those little books can be found in Rothbard's *The Mystery of Banking*, which was released in a handsome second edition in 2008. His book *America's Great Depression*, now in a fifth edition, applies Austrian business cycle theory to the worst economic downturn in American history. A collection called *The Austrian Theory of the Trade Cycle and Other Essays*, which contains essays by Rothbard, F. A. Hayek, and Ludwig von Mises, can likewise be read with profit regardless of your level of economic knowledge.

For economics in general, there is still no better introduction than Henry Hazlitt's classic *Economics in One Lesson.*

The great treasure trove of knowledge when it comes to the Austrian School of economics is Mises.org, the website of the Ludwig von Mises Institute. Hundreds of books are available there to read or print, as well as many thousands of articles for the average reader on every topic under the sun, the entire print runs of several scholarly journals, and (on the Media page) hundreds of hours of audio and video on some of the most important and fascinating issues of our time. It's all free. (All the books I recommend above, with the exception of *Economics in One Lesson,* are available there for free online reading, and three of them can be downloaded in audiobook format.)

My website, ThomasEWoods.com, links to the list of resources—including books (most readable online), articles, and audio and video files—that I compiled for people looking to learn more about the free market, sound money, and the Federal Reserve. The list, a full-fledged program of self-education, begins with elementary texts and works its way to the great treatises of the Austrian tradition: Mises' *Human Action* and Rothbard's *Man, Economy, and State.* Online and print study guides for both books are also available.

With so many people wrongly blaming "the free market" for America's economic woes, an understanding of sound economics is especially urgent today. If worse disasters are to be avoided, then those who believe in freedom and the free economy have no choice but to learn more about their position and how to defend it. Mises put it this way:

> Everyone carries a part of society on his shoulders; no one is relieved of his share of responsibility by others. And no one can find a safe way out for himself if society is sweeping toward destruction. Therefore, everyone, in his own interests, must thrust himself vigorously into the intellectual battle. None can stand aside with unconcern; the interest of everyone hangs on the result. Whether he chooses or not, every man is drawn into the

great historical struggle, the decisive battle into which our epoch has plunged us.

NOTES

Chapter 1: The Elephant in the Living Room

1. "Bush to Host Summit of Losers," Mish's Global Economic Trend Analysis, October 9, 2008, http://globaleconomicanalysis.blogspot.com/2008/10/bush-to-host-summit-of-losers.html.
2. Roger Runningen and Gregory Viscusi, "Bush Says He'll Host Summit Soon on Financial Crisis," Bloomberg.com, October 18, 2008, http://www.bloomberg.com/apps/news?pid=20601087&sid=ab8PtaRD 7KL8.
3. Sheryl Gay Stolberg, "Constituents Make Their Bailout Views Known," *New York Times*, September 25, 2008.
4. "House Members Voting 'Yes' on Bailout Received 54% More Money from Banks and Securities Firms than Members Voting 'No,'" MAP-Light.org, September 29, 2008, http://www.maplight.org/node /43109.
5. "Want Some Government Money? Apply Now!" November 12, 2008, http://blogs.abcnews.com/theworldnewser/2008/11/want-some-gover.html.
6. Bertrand Benoit, "Why Germans Just Hate to Spend, Spend, Spend," *Financial Times* [U.K.], November 28, 2008.
7. James K. Galbraith, interview with Deborah Solomon, *New York Times* (New York edition), November 2, 2008, MM13.

8. Henry Hazlitt, *What You Should Know About Inflation,* 2nd ed. (Princeton, N.J.: D. Van Nostrand, 1965), 18.

Chapter 2: How Government Created the Housing Bubble

1. Steven A. Holmes, "Fannie Mae Eases Credit to Aid Mortgage Lending," *New York Times,* September 30, 1999.
2. Ibid.
3. M. J. Wells, "Why the Mortgage Crisis Happened," *Investor's Business Daily,* October 29, 2008.
4. Stan J. Liebowitz, "Anatomy of a Train Wreck: Causes of the Mortgage Meltdown," Independent Policy Report, Independent Institute, October 3, 2008, 7.
5. Ibid., 8.
6. Ibid., 10.
7. Ibid., 14.
8. The material on Henry Cisneros relies on David Streitfeld and Gretchen Morgenson, "Building Flawed American Dreams," *New York Times,* October 18, 2008.
9. Liebowitz, "Anatomy of a Train Wreck," 15.
10. Ibid., 18.
11. Ibid., 11.
12. Carden delivered these remarks in Memphis, Tennessee, on October 14, 2008.
13. Liebowitz, "Anatomy of a Train Wreck," 12.
14. Cf. Ludwig von Mises, *Human Action,* Scholar's Edition (Auburn, Ala.: Ludwig von Mises Institute, 1998), 549–50.
15. Thanks to Michael Rozeff for this reference.
16. Chris Reidy, "Zero-down Mortgage Initiative by Bush Is Hit: Budget Office Says Plan Likely to Spur More Loan Defaults," *Boston Globe,* October 5, 2004.
17. Ben S. Bernanke, speech to the Independent Community Bankers of America National Convention, Las Vegas, Nevada, March 8, 2006; http://www.federalreserve.gov/BoardDocs/Speeches/2006/20060308/default.htm. Cited in Thornton, "The Economics of Housing Bubbles."
18. Jonathan McCarthy and Richard W. Peach, "Is there a 'Bubble' in the Housing Market Now?" Paper delivered at Eurobank EFG's conference on real estate, January 20, 2006; http://www.newyorkfed.org/research/economists/mccarthy/athens_bubble_paper.pdf. Thanks to Bob Murphy for this reference.
19. Testimony of Alan Greenspan, before the Special Committee on Aging, U.S. Senate, February 27, 2003; "U.S. Economy: Consumer Spending Shows Signs of Strengthening," Bloomberg.com, May 9, 2003, http://www.bloomberg.com/apps/news?pid=10000103&sid=a4ERjmO2X4io.

20. Antony Mueller, "Mr. Bailout," Mises.org, September 30, 2004; Antony P. Mueller, "Financial Cycles, Business Activity, and the Stock Market," *Quarterly Journal of Austrian Economics* 4 (Spring 2001): 14.

21. "'Greenspan Put' May Be Encouraging Complacency," *Financial Times*, December 8, 2000.

22. Quoted in Richard Rahn, "The Fed: Solution or Problem?" *Washington Times*, November 26, 2008.

Chapter 3: The Great Wall Street Bailout

1. NPR, "All Things Considered," March 2, 2007.

2. CNN Late Edition, March 16, 2008.

3. Bloomberg TV, May 17, 2007.

4. Associated Press, "Paulson Backs Bush Comment About Wall Street's 'Hangover,'" August 10, 2008.

5. Gary North, "The End of an Era," September 23, 2008, http://www.lewrockwell.com/north/north654.html.

6. Press Briefing by Dana Perino and Secretary of the Treasury Henry Paulson, September 15, 2008.

7. Edmund L. Andrews, Michael J. de la Merced, and Mary Williams Walsh, "Fed's $85 Billion Loan Rescues Insurer," *New York Times*, September 16, 2008.

8. Frank Shostak, "The Rescue Plan Will Delay Recovery," Mises.org, September 29, 2008.

9. Declan McCullagh, "Will U.S. Taxpayers Need a Bailout?" CBS News, October 15, 2008, http://www.cbsnews.com/stories/2008/10/14/politics/otherpeoplesmoney/main4522346.shtml.

10. David Brooks, "Revolt of the Nihilists," *New York Times*, September 29, 2008.

11. There's another way the ban hurts the very institutions it is supposed to help. Consider those firms that issue so-called credit default swaps (CDS), which pay buyers if a particular corporation should default on its bonds. One way these CDS-issuing firms could at least partly cover themselves if the corporation really did default was to short the stock of the firms they were insuring. If the firm should indeed default, its share price would drop precipitously, and thus anyone shorting it would profit. But if short-selling is banned, it becomes much riskier to issue CDS on the bonds of the vulnerable firms the government says it wants to assist. If firms can't guarantee themselves at least some money by shorting the stock of the insured company, they are much less likely to insure the company's bonds in the first place, and it will thus be harder for companies to borrow from investors. Robert P. Murphy, "Wall Street Plan Won't Aid Recovery," *San Diego Union-Tribune*, September 25, 2008. The question remains as to whether default on bonds is a properly insurable event in the first place, or whether CDS should be thought of as

risk-sharing mechanisms rather than insurance in the strict sense. In an economic environment in which a central bank can launch an artificial boom, credit insurance will inevitably wind up taking on systemic risks, and will come under severe strain when the bust comes. See Jesús Huerta de Soto, *Money, Bank Credit, and Economic Cycles*, trans. Melinda Stroup (Auburn, Ala.: Ludwig von Mises Institute, 2006), 598–600.

12. Gary Galles, "Don't Sell Short Selling Short," Mises.org, April 6, 2007.
13. Ibid.
14. On deposit insurance, see Murray N. Rothbard, *The Case Against the Fed* (Auburn, Ala.: Ludwig von Mises Institute, 1994), 134–37. The very word "insurance," when applied to the deposits in a fractional-reserve banking system, is a typical government Orwellianism, and is rather like fire insurance for a burning building.
15. Economist Arthur Wilmarth writes, "Studies have shown that the TBTF [too big to fail] policy confers a significant implicit subsidy on big U.S. banks, because (i) it allows them to pay below-average rates to depositors and other creditors, and (ii) it shields them from effective market discipline, despite their below-average capitalization and above-average risks." Arthur E. Wilmarth Jr., "Controlling Systemic Risk in an Era of Financial Consolidation," http://www.imf.org/external/np/leg/sem/2002/cdmfl/eng/wilmar.pdf. Thanks to Michael Rozeff for referring me to this paper.
16. Michael Rozeff gives an example: "Bank of America had 8.6% equity in 2007. Its deposits were 47% of capital. Much of these deposits are insured. Imagine that a man has $8,600 of his own money in a business, and he manages to borrow another $91,400 to deploy in the business. That's Bank of America. Now imagine that $47,000 of the total is insured by the government. No matter what he invests in, he does not have to worry about losing that $47,000, other than he may end up out of business. This man has an incentive to gamble with the money. If he loses, he loses $8,600 and his job. If he wins, the depositors do not get the winnings because deposits pay a fixed rate of interest. He and the stockholders get all the gravy. If he loses, most of the losses fall on the non-equity suppliers of capital. This is moral hazard." Michael S. Rozeff, "Deregulation Blunders and Moral Hazard," November 17, 2008, http://www.lewrockwell.com/rozeff/rozeff240.html.
17. Michael S. Malone, "The Pump-and-Dump Economy," *Wall Street Journal*, December 21, 2006.
18. V. V. Chari, Lawrence Christiano, and Patrick J. Kehoe, "Myths about the Financial Crisis of 2008," Working Paper 666, Federal Reserve Bank of Minneapolis Research Department, October 2008, available at http://www.minneapolisfed.org/research/WP/WP666.pdf. Criticisms of varying degrees of persuasiveness have been directed at this study, but

whatever the technical details, the point remains that while the rate of growth of credit slowed considerably, it still grew even during the "credit crunch."

19. Brian Love, "Credit Crunch? What Credit Crunch?" Reuters, December 11, 2008.

20. Statement of Secretary Henry M. Paulson Jr. on Financial Markets Update, Press Room, U.S. Department of the Treasurty, October 8, 2008, http://www.ustreas.gov/press/releases/hp1189.htm.

21. Rebecca Christie and Robert Schmidt, "Treasury to Invest in 'Healthy' Banks, Kashkari Says," Bloomberg.com, October 13, 2008, http://www.bloomberg.com/apps/news?pid=20601087&sid=aevZYw1y DiuA&refer=home.

22. Mark Landler, "U.S. Investing $250 Billion in Banks," *New York Times*, October 13, 2008.

23. "Chavez Says 'Comrade Bush' Turns Left in Crisis," Reuters, October 15, 2008, http://www.reuters.com/article/topNews/idUSTRE49F0K7 20081016.

24. David S. Hilzenrath and Glenn Kessler, "U.S. Seizes Control of AIG with $85 Billion Loan," *Washington Post*, September 17, 2008. The *Post* reported, "The Fed is using the emergency authority it was granted during the Great Depression. By law, the Fed can lend money to any individual, partnership or corporation in unusual and exigent circumstances, when the borrower cannot access funds in other ways. The power had not been exercised until March, when the Fed used it to rescue Bear Stearns." Thanks to Robert Higgs for this point.

25. Jeffrey A. Miron, "Why This Bailout Is as Bad as the Last One," CNN.com, October 14, 2008.

26. Associated Press, "Banks Using Government Money for Deals," *Boston Herald*, November 1, 2008.

27. Nicole Gelinas, "A Tale of Two Paulsons," *City Journal*, November 21, 2008, http://www.city-journal.org/2008/eon1121ng.html.

28. John Brinsley and Robert Schmidt, "Paulson Shifts Focus of Rescue to Consumer Lending," Bloomberg.com, November 12, 2008, http://www.bloomberg.com/apps/news?pid=20601087&sid=aVgfVZDn nFh4.

29. Robert Higgs, "Regime Uncertainty: Why the Great Depression Lasted So Long and Why Prosperity Resumed after the War," *Independent Review* 1 (Spring 1997): 561–90.

30. Robert Murphy, "Conservatives Should Oppose Corporate Welfare," Townhall.com, September 27, 2008. Any existing credit freeze, agrees Jeffrey Miron, is "likely due to Wall Street's hope of a bailout: bankers will not sell their lousy assets for 20 cents on the dollar if the government might pay 30, 50, or 80 cents." Jeffrey A. Miron, "Bankruptcy, not Bailout, Is the Right Answer," CNN.com, September 29, 2008.

31. On the mismanagement of the Big Three, see Doron Levin and John Helyar, "'Already Bankrupt' GM Won't Be Rescued by U.S. Loan," Bloomberg.com, December 12, 2008, http://www.bloomberg.com/apps/news?pid=20601170&refer=home&sid=ai5KpbywxqiQ.

32. Vernon L. Smith, "There's No Easy Way Out of the Bubble," *Wall Street Journal*, October 9, 2008.

33. Edmund L. Andrews, "Fed Cuts Benchmark Rate to Near Zero," *New York Times*, December 17, 2008.

34. Thanks to Anthony Gregory for this point.

35. Lionel Robbins, *The Great Depression* (London: Macmillan, 1934), 73.

36. William Graham Sumner, "The Delusion of the Debtors," in *Sumner, The Forgotten Man and Other Essays,* ed. Albert Galloway Keller (New Haven: Yale University Press, 1918), 153, 170.

37. Hayek was developing a theory first described by Ludwig von Mises.

Chapter 4: How Government Causes the Boom-Bust Cycle

1. Standard & Poor's Home Price Values, September 2008.

2. John Williams compiles this data at his Shadow Government Statistics website, http://www.shadowstats.com.

3. Lionel Robbins, *The Great Depression* (London: Macmillan, 1934), 31.

4. Ibid., 16.

5. "The Austrian theory of the business cycle," writes Roger Garrison, "emerges straightforwardly from a simple comparison of savings-induced growth, which is sustainable, with a credit-induced boom, which is not. An increase in saving by individuals and a credit expansion orchestrated by the central bank set into motion market processes whose initial allocational effects on the economy's capital structure are similar. But the ultimate consequences of the two processes stand in stark contrast: Saving gets us genuine growth; credit expansion gets us boom and bust." Roger W. Garrison, "The Austrian Theory: A Summary," in *The Austrian Theory of the Trade Cycle and Other Essays*, comp. Richard M. Ebeling (Auburn, Ala.: Ludwig von Mises Institute, 1996 [1978]), 98–99.

6. Jörg Guido Hülsmann, *The Ethics of Money Production* (Auburn, Ala.: Ludwig von Mises Institute, 2008), 71.

7. Ludwig von Mises, *Human Action: A Treatise on Economics*, Scholar's Edition (Auburn, Ala.: Ludwig von Mises Institute, 1998), 557. Mises' treatise was first published in 1949 by Yale University Press. Economist Robert Murphy elaborates on Mises' house example in Robert P. Murphy, "An Open Letter to Gary Becker re: Depressions," Mises.org, November 24, 2008, http://mises.org/story/3220.

8. "Once costs have begun to rise it would require a continuous increase in the rate of increase of credit to prevent the thing coming to disaster. But that itself, as we have seen in the great postwar inflations, would even-

tually generate panic. Sooner or later the initial errors are discovered. And then starts a reverse rush for liquidity. The stock exchange collapses. There is a stoppage of new issues. Production in the industries producing capital goods slows down. The boom is at an end." Robbins, *The Great Depression*, 41–42.

9. The Austrian theory "shows how, when the boom has collapsed, there exist dislocations and disproportionalities in the world of industry, the wreckage of false expectations, which monetary manipulation is not likely to remove." Robbins, *The Great Depression*, 43.

10. John Maynard Keynes, *The General Theory of Employment, Interest, and Money* (New York: Harcourt Trade, 1964 [1936]), 322.

11. "When measures to 'keep the boom going' are applied repeatedly," writes Antony Mueller, "more profound transformations of the capital structure will occur. This will make the economy less and less efficient, leading to a bust and, finally, to economic paralysis." Antony P. Mueller, "Financial Cycles, Business Activity, and the Stock Market," *Quarterly Journal of Austrian Economics* 4 (Spring 2001): 9.

12. F. A. Hayek, *Prices and Production and Other Works*, ed. Joseph T. Salerno (Auburn, Ala.: Ludwig von Mises Institute, 2008), 6–7.

13. Robbins, *The Great Depression*, 37.

14. Peter D. Schiff, *Crash Proof: How to Profit from the Coming Economic Collapse* (New York: Wiley, 2007), 88–89.

15. Gene Callahan and Roger W. Garrison, "Does Austrian Business Cycle Theory Help Explain the Dot-Com Boom and Bust?" *Quarterly Journal of Austrian Economics* 6 (Summer 2003): 89.

16. Mises, *Human Action*, 551. Emphasis added.

17. "Tories Accuse Darling of 'Giant Con' Over Plans to Raise Taxes after Recession Is Over," *Daily Mail* (U.K.), November 13, 2008.

18. Edmund L. Andrews, "Fed Cuts Benchmark Rate to Near Zero," *New York Times*, December 17, 2008.

19. Callahan and Garrison, "Dot-Com Boom and Bust," 86.

20. Ibid., 85.

21. Hans F. Sennholz, "The Fed is Culpable," Mises.org, November 11, 2002.

22. De Soto argues that "uninterrupted stock market growth never indicates favorable economic conditions. Quite the contrary: all such growth provides the most unmistakable sign of credit expansion unbacked by real savings, expansion which feeds an artificial boom that will invariably culminate in a severe stock market crisis." Jesus Huerta de Soto, *Money, Bank Credit, and Economic Cycles*, trans. Melinda D. Straup (Auburn, Ala.: Ludwig von Mises Institute, 2006), 462. He thus amplifies Fritz Machlup's contention that "if it were not for the elasticity of bank credit, which has often been regarded as such a good thing, the boom in security values could not last for any length of time. In the absence of infla-

tionary credit the funds available for lending to the public for security purchases would soon be exhausted." Fritz Machlup, *The Stock Market, Credit, and Capital Formation*, 92, trans. Vera C. Smith (London: William Hodge and Co., 1940), 92.

23. Callahan and Garrison, "Dot Com Boom and Bust," 87.

24. The technical details referred to here are explained in later chapters.

25. Mark Thornton, "The Economics of Housing Bubbles," in *Housing America: Building Out of a Crisis*, ed. Randall G. Holcombe and Benjamin Powell (New Brunswick, N.J.: Transaction, forthcoming July 2009).

26. Thanks to Mark Thornton for this point.

27. Mainstream economics, it should be pointed out, can scarcely be said to possess any capital theory at all, much less one that conceives of capital as a series of time-consuming stages from higher order to lower order. Capital, to economists trained in that tradition, is a homogenous lump. As a result, it is impossible for the average economist even to perceive an Austrian-style boom and bust when it occurs. "If one were, for instance, to aggregate heterogeneous capital goods into 'capital,' the complex relationships among capital goods would be lost," write economists Gerald O'Driscoll and Mario Rizzo. Gerald P. O'Driscoll and Mario Rizzo, *The Economics of Time and Ignorance*, 2nd ed. (London: Routledge, 1996), 190. Keynes expressly disregarded the structure of production in chapter four of his *General Theory*, and in a 1937 article actually *boasted* of having separated macroeconomics from capital theory—thereby assuming away everything that should be of interest to the economist studying business cycles.

28. For the statistics, see Benjamin Powell, "Explaining Japan's Recession," *Quarterly Journal of Austrian Economics* 5 (Summer 2002): 48.

29. William Bonner with Addison Wiggin, *Financial Reckoning Day* (New York: John Wiley & Sons, 2004), 237.

30. Powell, "Explaining Japan's Recession," 39.

31. Frank Shostak, "Are Fannie and Freddie Too Big to Fail?" Mises.org, September 17, 2008. To force the Japanese to spend, figures like Milton Friedman and Ben Bernanke suggested, in the words of economist Mark Thornton, that "the central bank should simply print up unlimited amounts of money, that the bank threaten consumers (who are hoarding their own money) with ever-increasing levels of inflation, or that the central bank purchase worthless stocks, corporate bonds, real estate, and even directly fund government expenditures." Mark Thornton, "Apoplithorismosphobia," *Quarterly Journal of Austrian Economics* 6 (Winter 2003): 11n5.

32. Quoted in Thornton, "Apoplithorismosphobia," 14.

33. Quoted in ibid.

34. Mises, *Human Action*, 583.

35. Quoted in Brian M. Carney, "Bernanke is Fighting the Last War," *Wall Street Journal*, October 18, 2008.
36. Paul Krugman, "Fear Itself," *New York Times*, September 30, 2001.

Chapter 5: Great Myths about the Great Depression

1. In this context it is worth noting the work of Christina Romer, who suggests that to some extent the severity of the cyclical swings in the nineteenth century as opposed to the twentieth, especially since the 1940s, is an artifact of the statistical measures used. See Christina D. Romer, "Is the Stabilization of the Postwar Economy a Figment of the Data?" *American Economic Review* 76 (June 1986): 314–34; idem, "Remeasuring Business Cycles," *Journal of Economic History* 54 (September 1994): 573–609. On the nineteenth century, see also H. A. Scott Trask, "William Graham Sumner: Monetary Theorist," *Quarterly Journal of Austrian Economics* 8 (Summer 2005): 35–54.
2. For this criticism of the Second Bank of the United States, see Murray N. Rothbard, *The Panic of 1819: Reactions and Policies* (New York: Columbia University Press, 1962), ch. V.
3. William M. Gouge, *A Short History of Paper Money and Banking in the United States* (New York: Augustus M. Kelley, 1968 [1833]), 83.
4. Rothbard, *The Panic of 1819*, 21.
5. Ibid., 182.
6. William Leggett, *Democratick Editorials: Essays in Jacksonian Political Economy*, ed. Lawrence H. White (Indianapolis, Ind.: Liberty Press, 1984), 93.
7. Ibid., 98.
8. Ibid., 97.
9. Ibid., 116.
10. Jesús Huerta de Soto, *Money, Bank Credit, and Economic Cycles*, trans. Melinda A. Stroup (Auburn, Ala.: Ludwig von Mises Institute, 2006), 484–85.
11. H. A. Scott Trask, "Reflation in American History," October 31, 2003, http://www.mises.org/articles.aspx?AuthorId=161.
12. Murray N. Rothbard, *A History of Money and Banking in the United States: The Colonial Era to World War II*, ed. Joseph T. Solerno (Auburn, Ala.: Ludwig von Mises Institute, 2002), 135.
13. Michael S. Rozeff, "The Panic of 2008 and Financial Socialization," October 20, 2008, http://www.lewrockwell.com/rozeff/rozeff231.html. Rozeff writes, "The boom of 1869–1873 involved a banking system that created money backed by government bonds. The Fed does the same today. In both cases, it also involved congressional stimulus. In the 1860s, it was railroad subsidies. In this century, it was a variety of measures to stimulate house construction and to absorb the mortgage credits via government-sponsored institutions like Fannie Mae and Freddie Mac."

14. Jeremy Atack and Peter Passel, *A New Economic View of American History* (New York: W.W. Norton, 1979), 523. Correcting for population growth, the increase in manufacturing employment per year is modest, but since productivity was increasing and fewer people were therefore needed to produce the same number of goods, any increase in the amount of employment in manufacturing indicated a significantly expanding and healthy manufacturing sector. (Thanks to Tom DiLorenzo for this reference.)

15. Rothbard, *A History of Money and Banking in the United States*, 154–55. Emphasis in original.

16. Milton Friedman and Anna Schwartz, *A Monetary History of the United States, 1867–1960* (Princeton: Princeton University Press, 1971), 87–88; quoted in Joseph T. Salerno, "An Austrian Taxonomy of Deflation— With Applications to the U.S.," *Quarterly Journal of Austrian Economics* 6 (Winter 2003): 89.

17. William Graham Sumner, *A History of American Currency* (New York: Henry Holt, 1874), 172.

18. Useful statistics on monetary expansion, depression, and recovery can be found in Kenneth Weiher, *America's Search for Economic Stability: Monetary and Fiscal Policy Since 1913* (New York: Twayne, 1992), 26–37.

19. Robert Aaron Gordon, *Economic Instability and Growth: The American Record* (New York: Harper and Row, 1974), 21–22, cited in Salerno, "An Austrian Taxonomy of Deflation," 95–96.

20. Robert A. Degen, *The American Monetary System: A Concise Survey of Its Evolution Since 1896* (Lexington, Mass.: D.C. Heath, 1987), 41.

21. On Japan, see Benjamin M. Anderson, *Economics and the Public Welfare: A Financial and Economic History of the United States, 1914–1946* (Indianapolis: Liberty Press, 1979 [1949]), 88–89, 90.

22. Ibid., 92.

23. For comprehensive refutations of this widespread misinterpretation of events, see Murray N. Rothbard, *America's Great Depression*, 4th ed. (New York: Richardson & Snyder, 1983) and Melchior Palyi, *The Twilight of Gold, 1914–1936: Myths and Realities* (Chicago: Henry Regnery, 1972).

24. Percy L. Greaves Jr., *Understanding the Dollar Crisis* (Boston: Western Islands, 1973), 222–23.

25. F. A. Hayek wrote, "But even if the money supply is increased just sufficiently to prevent a fall in prices, it must have basically the same effect on the structure of production as any...expansion in the quantity of money not 'justified' by an increase in output." Quoted in Mark Skousen, *The Structure of Production* (New York: New York University Press, 1990), 355–56.

26. This figure comes from Professor Joseph T. Salerno, who uses Murray Rothbard's data but excludes from Rothbard's money supply figures the

cash surrender value of life insurance policies, a controversial (but hardly unheard of) factor that affected Rothbard's inflation statistics only slightly in any case. See Joseph T. Salerno, "Money and Gold in the 1920s and 1930s: An Austrian View," *Ideas on Liberty* 49 (October 1999), 31–40. This important essay has recently been made available online: http://www.fee.org/publications/the-freeman/article.asp?aid= 4942

27. Statistics are available in Rothbard, *America's Great Depression*, principally in chapters 4 and 5; see also Greaves, *Understanding the Dollar Crisis*, Lecture VI. Rothbard's interpretation of the 1920s has not been without controversy, but attempted refutations of his position fail. Joe Salerno disaggregates the data to uncover those factors influencing the money supply that were controlled by the Fed and those that were uncontrolled. He finds that by and large the Fed did try to inflate the money supply, but was frustrated by individuals who refused to spend and banks that refused to lend. Salerno concludes that "the Fed's monetary policy, except for very brief periods in 1929 and 1936–1937 when it turns mildly disinflationist, was consistently and unremittingly inflationist in the 1920s and 1930s. This inflationism was the cause of the Great Depression and one of the reasons why it was so protracted." Salerno, "Money and Gold in the 1920s and 1930s: An Austrian View."

28. Rothbard, *America's Great Depression*, 148.

29. Mark Thornton, "Mises vs. Fisher on Money, Method, and Prediction: The Case of the Great Depression," Ludwig von Mises Institute Working Paper, December 19, 2006, 9.

30. Ibid., 9–10.

31. Ibid., 14.

32. Ibid.

33. "FDR's Disputed Legacy," *Time*, February 1, 1982, 23; cited in Lawrence W. Reed, "Great Myths of the Great Depression," rev. ed., Mackinac Center for Public Policy, 2005, 6.

34. On the conference, see Rothbard, *America's Great Depression*, 276–77.

35. In a fireside chat on October 22, 1933, for instance, FDR explained: "I repeat what I have said on many occasions, that ever since last March the definite policy of the Government has been to restore commodity price levels." Quoted in Greaves, *Understanding the Dollar Crisis*, 237.

36. Robbins, *The Great Depression*, 75.

37. Harold L. Cole and Lee E. Ohanian, "New Deal Policies and the Persistence of the Great Depression: A General Equilibrium Analysis," *Journal of Political Economy* 112 (August 2004): 813.

38. Rothbard, *History of Money and Banking*, 103. Some people have criticized the Fed for failing to pump more money into the economy at a time when the money supply was contracting, but it wasn't for lack of trying. Contrary to popular belief, the Fed tried to inflate the money supply, but in such uncertain times the banks were understandably reluc-

tant to lend out the new money, and many people preferred to hold their money in cash instead of putting it in the bank where it could serve as the base for additional layers of money creation.

39. Salerno, "Money and Gold in the 1920s and 1930s: An Austrian View"; see also Richard K. Vedder and Lowell E. Gallaway, *Out of Work: Unemployment and Government in Twentieth-Century America* (New York: Holmes & Meier, 1993), ch. 7.

40. Paul Krugman, "Franklin Delano Obama?" *New York Times*, November 10, 2008.

41. See Robert Higgs, *Depression, War, and Cold War* (New York: Oxford University Press, 2006); see my distillation in Thomas E. Woods Jr., *33 Questions About American History You're Not Supposed to Ask* (New York: Crown Forum, 2007), 97–105. On a related note, economist George Reisman wrote in 1996, "People believed they were prosperous in World War II because they were piling up large amounts of unspendable income—in the form of paper money and government bonds. They confused this accumulation of paper assets with real wealth. Incredibly, most economic statisticians and historians make the same error when they measure the standard of living of World War II by the largely unspendable 'national income' of the period." George Reisman, *Capitalism* (Ottawa, Ill.: Jameson Books, 1996), 262.

42. Jon Basil Utley first devised this thought experiment.

Chapter 6: Money

1. Leverage, the practice whereby firms borrowing money to make an investment they hope will appreciate at a greater rate than the interest the firms are paying to borrow, is artificially encouraged in excess by the Fed's easy money policy. According to Thorsten Polleit of the Frankfurt School of Finance and Management, "The outstanding expansion of credit derivatives, heaped upon a giant paper-credit pyramid, has been stimulated to a great extent by central banks' chronic low interest rates, having made investors search for yield pick-up and ignore credit and market risks." "Greater use of financial leverage accompanies the boom," writes professor of finance Michael Rozeff. "More firms expect profits from investing in long-term assets since the prices of this class of assets rise the most. By financing them with the cheapest debt, which is short-term debt, the credit creation encourages a duration mismatch: borrowing short and lending (or buying) long. This practice violates the standard and conservative financing rule, which is to match the maturities (or durations) of loans with the maturities (or durations) of the assets they finance." Cheap credit and an implicit bailout guarantee from the Fed encourage the very kind of leveraging, excess risk, and unjustified optimism that so often characterize the boom phase of the business cycle. It is these indispensable ingredients that need to be targeted and eliminated. See Thorsten Polleit,

"Confidence Is Leaving the Fiat Money System," Mises.org, October 10, 2008; Michael S. Rozeff, "Understanding Recession," October 21, 2008, http://www.lewrockwell.com/rozeff/rozeff232.html.

On the subject of risk, a caveat may be in order. The risk modeling that some firms adopted turned out to be seriously flawed, underestimating risk and leaving institutions unable to cover themselves in the event of financial catastrophe. The argument has been advanced, though, that in the case of AIG it may not have been the risk models themselves that caused the problem. Although the full story is not yet known, it looks as if the risk models that consultant Gary Gorton constructed for AIG may not have been responsible for the company's demise. What sank AIG were the demands by large clients like Goldman Sachs for more and more collateral to be put up against the financial instruments it had issued. In other words, writes the Pacific Research Institute's Robert Murphy, "Gorton's models may still prove to be fairly accurate; AIG was not crippled by a string of unexpected credit events (and consequent payouts). What actually happened is that the holders of CDS issued by AIG became scared about AIG's ability to honor its contracts, and AIG could not continue to operate while satisfying all of the growing calls to put up more collateral against these outstanding time bombs. In short, AIG was plagued by illiquidity, not necessarily by insolvency. It is true that AIG executives failed to adequately prepare for this contingency, but it nonetheless removes some of the mystery behind its failure when we realize that AIG may very well have correctly assessed the risk of its positions—it just failed to correctly predict how its *customers* would assess this risk, in the midst of a global financial panic and also during a period when there was a 'credit crunch' among large institutions." Robert P. Murphy, "Did Deregulated Derivatives Cause the Financial Crisis?" *The Freeman*, forthcoming.

2. Robert P. Murphy, *The Politically Incorrect Guide™ to Capitalism* (Washington, D.C.: Regnery, 2007), 88. Ludwig von Mises wrote, "It is certainly more plausible to take for granted that the immediate advantages conferred by indirect exchange were recognized by the acting parties than to assume that the whole image of a society trading by means of money was conceived by a genius and...made obvious to the rest of the people by persuasion." Ludwig von Mises, *Human Action: A Treatise on Economics*, Scholar's edition (Auburn, Ala.: Ludwig von Mises Institute, 1998), 403.

3. On this process, see Murray N. Rothbard, *What Has Government Done to Our Money?* 4th ed. (Auburn, Ala.: Ludwig von Mises Institute, 1990).

4. "At no time in history," writes monetary theorist Jörg Guido Hülsmann, "has paper money been produced in a competitive market setting. Whenever and wherever it came into being, it existed only because the court

and the police suppressed the natural alternatives." Jörg Guido Hüls-mann, *The Ethics of Money Production* (Auburn, Ala.: Ludwig von Mises Institute, 2008), 55.

5. Henry Hazlitt, *What You Should Know About Inflation*, 2nd ed. (Princeton, N.J.: D. Van Nostrand, 1965), 25–26.

6. Joseph A. Schumpeter, *History of Economic Analysis* (New York: Oxford University Press, 1954), 405–406. Thanks to Mark Thornton for this reference.

7. The ensuing discussion follows Rothbard, *What Has Government Done to Our Money?*

8. Operating on a fractional-reserve basis was not always smiled upon by the law. The act of depositing money in a demand deposit at a bank was considered as no different from entrusting someone with the safekeeping of valuables. Someone who stores his property in a warehouse for safekeeping does not forfeit his ownership or control of those goods, and anyone failing to return them on demand would be guilty of embezzlement or theft.

Research by Spain's most prominent Austrian economist, Jesús Huerta de Soto, discovered that Roman law, one of the building blocks of Western civilization, distinguished between time and demand deposits, and absolutely forbade the lending out of demand deposits. The legal status of the fractional-reserve principle became more ambiguous in the modern period, and by the mid–nineteenth century a series of important cases established it as an allowable practice in England. The American banking system by and large followed the principles of the English system. On banking and Roman law, see Jesús Huerta de Soto, *Money, Bank Credit, and Economic Cycles*, trans. Melinda A. Stroup (Auburn, Ala.: Ludwig von Mises Institute, 2006), ch. 1.

9. On all this, see Murray N. Rothbard, *The Mystery of Banking*, 2nd ed. (Auburn, Ala.: Ludwig von Mises Institute, 2008).

10. Gene Smiley, *Rethinking the Great Depression* (Chicago: Ivan R. Dee, 2002), 37–38.

11. Ibid., 39.

12. Jesús Huerta de Soto points out that because of the instability of fractional-reserve banking on a free market, such a system invariably gives rise to great and perhaps irresistible pressure to establish a central bank to coordinate all the banks' inflation and help keep them all solvent without forcing them to cease fractional-reserve activity altogether. The point of the central bank is to alleviate pressures that the free market would otherwise impose. De Soto, *Money, Bank Credit, and Economic Cycles*, 638.

13. This discussion of the banking system and the Fed derives from the explanation in Thomas E. Woods Jr., *The Church and the Market: A Catholic Defense of the Free Economy* (Lanham, Md.: Lexington, 2005), 87–94.

14. When we read in the news that the Fed has "lowered interest rates," the writer is referring to something called the federal funds rate, the interest rate at which banks lend to each other. The Fed lowers this rate by the open market operations we have seen here, in this case pumping additional reserves into the system. The additional reserves give the banks additional funds to lend, and these additional funds lower the federal funds rate. The Fed injects reserves in an amount it estimates will lower the federal funds rate to whatever target rate it seeks. In the past the Fed has also used various price indexes as targeting mechanisms. What matters for our purposes is not all the technical talk of "targeting," but the injections of reserves themselves.

15. Perhaps an even better definition of inflation is an increase in the supply of money greater than would occur on the free market. This definition is preferred by Professor Hülsmann. See Hülsmann, *The Ethics of Money Production*, 85.

16. Hülsmann, *The Ethics of Money Production*, 182–83.

17. Jörg Guido Hülsmann, "Optimal Monetary Policy," *Quarterly Journal of Austrian Economics* 6 (Winter 2003): 54.

18. Murray N. Rothbard, *Man, Economy, and State: A Treatise on Economic Principles* (Princeton, N.J.: D. Van Nostrand, 1962), 40–49.

19. This example comes from economist Frank Shostak, whose emphasis on real savings as the basis of credit is a leitmotif of his writing.

20. As Mises explained, artificial credit creation "cannot increase the supply of real goods. It merely brings about a rearrangement. It diverts capital investment away from the course prescribed by the state of economic wealth and market conditions. It causes production to pursue paths which it would not follow unless the economy were to acquire an increase in material goods. As a result, the upswing lacks a solid base. It is *not* real prosperity. It is *illusory* prosperity. It did not develop from an increase in economic wealth. Rather, it arose because the credit expansion created the illusion of such an increase. Sooner or later it must become apparent that this economic situation is built on sand." Ludwig von Mises, *The Causes of the Economic Crisis, and Other Essays Before and After the Great Depression* (Auburn, Ala.: Ludwig von Mises Institute, 2006), 162. This book was originally published in 1978 as *On the Manipulation of Money and Credit*.

21. On this point, see Walter Block, "The Gold Standard: A Critique of Friedman, Mundell, Hayek, Greenspan," *Managerial Finance* 25 (May 1999): 16–19.

22. Hülsmann, *The Ethics of Money Production*, 80n34.

23. Quoted in Hans F. Sennholz, *Age of Inflation* (Belmont, Mass.: Western Islands, 1979), 19.

24. On the fallacy of "price stabilization," see Rothbard, *Man, Economy, and State*, 741–44.

25. Henry Hazlitt, *Man vs. the Welfare State* (New Rochelle, N.Y.: Arlington House, 1969), 163. First emphasis in original; second emphasis added.

Chapter 7: What Now?

1. On this subject, see Murray N. Rothbard, *Man, Economy, and State: A Treatise on Economic Principles* (Princeton, N.J.: D. Van Nostrand, 1962), 343–45.
2. Including intermediate stages of production in GDP is criticized as "double counting," but whether it's "double counting" depends on what it is you're trying to count.
3. John Stuart Mill, *Principles of Political Economy* (New York: A. M. Kelley, 1999), 74.
4. Murray N. Rothbard, *America's Great Depression*, 4th ed. (New York: Richardson & Snyder, 1983), 277.
5. As James Mill said, "The demand of a nation is always equal to the produce of a nation. This indeed must be so; for what is the demand of a nation? The demand of a nation is exactly its power of purchasing. But what is its power of purchasing? The extent undoubtedly of its annual produce." James Mill, *On the Underconsumption and Overproduction Fallacies*, ed. George Reisman (Laguna Hills, Calif.: Jefferson School of Philosophy, Economics, and Psychology, 2000), 8–9. This material is excerpted from Mill's *Commerce Defended* of 1808.
6. See Henry Hazlitt, *The Failure of the "New Economics": An Analysis of the Keynesian Fallacies* (Princeton, N.J.: D. Van Nostrand, 1959), 32–43. If you wish to observe one of the great twentieth-century cranks rebutted line by line, this book is indispensable. As a point-by-point refutation of Keynes's *General Theory* it unfortunately lacks an overall critique of Keynes's system, but all the same it is the most devastating demolition of one intellectual by another I have ever seen anywhere, and it will give you a new and healthy contempt for anyone who points to Keynes as an economist, or as having anything worthwhile to say on economics. For a more general critique of Keynes, see George Reisman, *Capitalism*, (Ottawa, Ill.: Jameson Books, 1996), ch. 18.
7. Mill, *On the Underconsumption and Overproduction Fallacies*, 5–6.
8. This analogy comes from Peter Schiff.
9. Steven Landsburg, "Why Secretary Paulson's Plan to Bail Out the Financial Industry Needs a Better Explanation," TheAtlantic.com, September 22, 2008, http://thecurrent.theatlantic.com/archives/2008/09/not-buying-it.php.
10. Jeffrey A. Miron, "Bankruptcy, Not Bailout, Is the Right Answer," CNN.com, September 29, 2008, http://www.cnn.com/2008/POLITICS/09/29/miron.bailout.
11. Robert Higgs, "The Trillion-Dollar Defense Budget Is Already Here,"

http://www.independent.org/newsroom/article.asp?id=1941.

12. John Morton Blum, *From the Morgenthau Diaries: Years of Crisis, 1928–1938* (Boston: Houghton Mifflin, 1959), 70; cited in Lawrence W. Reed, "Great Myths of the Great Depression," rev. ed., Mackinac Center for Public Policy, 2005, 15.

13. Ron Paul, *The Revolution: A Manifesto* (New York: Grand Central, 2008), 150.

14. Mark Pittman, Bob Ivry, and Alison Fitzgerald, "Fed Defies Transparency Aim in Refusal to Disclose," November 10, 2008, http://www.bloomberg.com/apps/news?pid=20601087&sid=aatlky_cH.t Y&refer=worldwide.

15. Judy Shelton, "Loose Money and the Roots of the Crisis," *Wall Street Journal*, September 30, 2008.

16. Henry Hazlitt, *What You Should Know About Inflation*, 2nd ed. (Princeton, N.J.: D. Van Nostrand, 1965), 29.

17. For the defects of the classical gold standard from a free-market point of view, see Jörg Guido Hülsmann, *The Ethics of Money Production* (Auburn, Ala.: Ludwig von Mises Institute, 2008), 209–13. For a case study of private coinage, see George Selgin, *Good Money: Birmingham Button Makers, the Royal Mint, and the Beginnings of Modern Coinage, 1775–1821* (Ann Arbor, Mich.: University of Michigan Press, 2008). We should not expect hundreds of monies to exist under a system of monetary freedom; for a money to serve its purpose it needs to be widely marketable and easily recognized, and that becomes more difficult to do the greater the variety of monies. On its own the market has given us personal computers that are by and large compatible with each other and electrical products with plugs of the same size. Since people want that kind of standardization, the market gives it to them. The same would be true of money.

18. F. A. Hayek, "Toward a Free Market Monetary System," *Journal of Libertarian Studies* 3 (Spring 1979): 1–8. These remarks were first delivered on November 10, 1977, at the Gold and Monetary Conference in New Orleans, Louisiana.

19. Hülsmann, *The Ethics of Money Production*, 241.

20. Hazlitt, *What You Should Know About Inflation*, 58–61; Murray N. Rothbard, *The Mystery of Banking*, 2nd ed. (Auburn, Ala.: Ludwig von Mises Institute, 2008 [1983]), 261–68. Economist George Reisman describes his own plan in "The Path to Sound Money": http://mises.org/multimedia/mp3/MU2007/61-Reisman.mp3.

21. See Peter D. Schiff, *Crash Proof: How to Profit from the Coming Economic Collapse* (New York: Wiley, 2007), 213–14. In addition to Schiff's comments, the Free Lakota Bank is one among numerous recent examples of private money alternatives that have already come into existence.

22. On the 1990s, see Mark Thornton, "Who Predicted the Bubble? Who Predicted the Crash?" *Independent Review* 9 (Summer 2004): 5–30.

INDEX

ABOUT THE AUTHOR

Thomas E. Woods Jr. (B.A., Harvard; M.A., M.Phil., Ph.D., Columbia) is a senior fellow at the Ludwig von Mises Institute in Auburn, Alabama. He is the author of nine books, including *Who Killed the Constitution?: The Fate of American Liberty from World War I to George W. Bush* (with Kevin R. C. Gutzman), *33 Questions About American History You're Not Supposed to Ask*, and the *New York Times* bestseller *The Politically Incorrect Guide™ to American History*.

Woods won the $50,000 first prize in the 2006 Templeton Enterprise Awards for *The Church and the Market: A Catholic Defense of the Free Economy*. Columbia University Press released his critically acclaimed 2004 book *The Church Confronts Modernity* in paperback in 2007. His books have been translated into Italian, Spanish, Polish, German, Portuguese, Croatian, Korean, and Chinese.

Woods edited and wrote the introduction to four additional books: *The Political Writings of Rufus Choate*, Murray N. Rothbard's *The Be-*

trayal of the American Right, We Who Dared to Say No to War: American Antiwar Writing from 1812 to Now (with Murray Polner), and Orestes Brownson's 1875 classic *The American Republic*. He is also the author of *Beyond Distributism*, part of the Acton Institute's Christian Social Thought Series.

Woods's writing has appeared in dozens of popular and scholarly periodicals, including *Investor's Business Daily, American Historical Review, Christian Science Monitor, Quarterly Journal of Austrian Economics, Modern Age, American Studies, Journal of Markets & Morality, New Oxford Review, University Bookman, Independent Review, Human Rights Review,* and *Journal des Economistes et des Etudes Humaines*. He is the editor of the *Journal of Libertarian Studies* and a contributing editor of *The American Conservative*. A contributor to half a dozen encyclopedias, Woods is co-editor of *Exploring American History: From Colonial Times to 1877*, an 11-volume encyclopedia.

Woods has appeared on FOX News Channel's *Hannity & Colmes, FOX & Friends,* and *The Big Story with John Gibson,* as well as on MSNBC's *Scarborough Country* and C-SPAN's *Book TV*. He has been a guest on over 200 radio programs, including *FOX News Live with Alan Colmes,* the *G. Gordon Liddy Show,* and the *Michael Medved Show*. In 2008 he hosted a 13-program miniseries on EWTN, the global Catholic television network.

Woods lives in Auburn, Alabama, with his wife and three daughters, and maintains a website at ThomasEWoods.com.